The Alhambra and the Alcázar of Seville: The History of the Famous
Fortresses Constructed by the Moors in Spain

By Charles River Editors

Alhambra from San Nicolas Square

About Charles River Editors

Charles River Editors provides superior editing and original writing services across the digital publishing industry, with the expertise to create digital content for publishers across a vast range of subject matter. In addition to providing original digital content for third party publishers, we also republish civilization's greatest literary works, bringing them to new generations of readers via ebooks.

Sign up here to receive updates about free books as we publish them, and visit Our Kindle Author Page to browse today's free promotions and our most recently published Kindle titles.

Introduction

The Alhambra

Tucked away on the crest of the Al-Sabika Hill in Granada of Andalusia, Spain, just left of the babbling stream of the Darro River, sits a majestic structure overlooking the charming city and mystical meadows of La Vega. This palatial fortress and the fabled Alhambra are one and the same. To those that have seen it in its full glory, this was heaven on earth itself. Many were quick to fall under the spell of its breathtaking beauty, with its admirers lovingly dubbing it "a pearl set in emeralds."

At one point in time, this place had been decked out with a network of captivating castles, heavenly homes and gorgeous gardens, and a handsome military fortress envied by the city's neighboring kingdoms. This was none other than Alhambra, once so enchanting that a countless number of those who visited the place in its heyday praised it as a true paradise on earth. Today, this historic complex has become the setting and inspiration for a host of books, music, movies, and other works of art and literature, such as Washington Irving's *Tales of Alhambra*, and Marcel L'Herbier's cinematic masterpiece, *El Dorado*. A main asteroid belt has even been named after the legendary place.

The exquisite work of art continues to be beloved, so much so that a campaign in 2007 attracted an estimated 5,000 hopefuls to the site. There, the thousands laced their fingers together and formed a ring around the spectacular fortress stretching 1.5 miles long, in hopes of cementing the landmark's place among the "New 7 Wonders of the World." Astounding aesthetics aside, the rich tapestry of history that unfolded within the walls of the centuries-old palatial paradise is truly what makes Alhambra one of the classic, timeless gems in all of Europe.

Even if one were to discount security and the Spanish royals who reside here seasonally, legend has it that the Alcázar is never truly uninhabited. Take a post-midnight stroll through the colonnades or the baths, and listen closely, insist mystics, and one will hear the spine-tingling sniffling, harrowing whimpers, and wretched weeping of the hapless souls who met their demise at the hands of Pedro the Cruel, Peter I of Castile, one of the many builders and tenants of this bewitching place. The vicious and volatile wrath of the cruel monarch knew no bounds, and his victims, no numbers. Some say these cries belong to the young maidens who were burnt at the stake for no other reason than rejecting Pedro's romantic advances. Others say they come from the spirit of Eleanor of Guzman, the mistress of Pedro's father, Alfonso XI of Castile, and one of Pedro's first kills. Or perhaps they come from all of Pedro's victims, cursed by their violent deaths to roam the Alcázar in perpetuity.

Luis Garcia's picture of a 16th century statue of Pedro the Cruel

A depiction of Alfonso XI of Castile in Froissart's chronicles

Like Alfonso, Pedro smote anyone who opposed, threatened, or displeased him in any way, no matter how trivial. Eleanor, however, was one Pedro executed out of sheer vengeance. When Alfonso was still in power, the philandering sovereign unabashedly neglected his wife, Maria of Portugal, along with their children, Fernando and Pedro, treasuring instead his relationship with Eleanor, and the 10 children she bore him. Eleanor was revered by state officials and nobility by default, and acted as Alfonso's de facto consort, dipping her toes and pitching in her 2 cents to all matters of the state. 8-year-old Fadrique Alfonso, among the brood of 10, was appointed Grand Master of the Order of Santiago, a Christian order of Spanish knights that aimed to vanquish Spanish Saracens and guard the pilgrims that trekked to the shrine of the *Santiago de Compostela* (more on him later).

Shortly after Alfonso's death in late March of 1350, courtesy of the plague, 16-year-old Pedro, working in tandem with the embittered dowager, accused Eleanor of stirring up a revolt, confined her to the dungeons, and had her executed in the city of Talavera de la Reina a year later. Apart from the multiple assertions of Eleanor's innocence falling on deaf ears, the helpless captive was subjected to a slow and hideous death. Some say her executioners crudely sliced her neck open with a butcher's cleaver. Others say she was left tethered to a post with the cord pinching her neck, left to starve under the unforgiving sun until she eventually perished from exposure days later.

Even Pedro's chief advisers and the formerly untouchable aristocracy were apparently reduced to quaking sycophants and bootlickers in his presence, for they, too, were expendable in the king's eyes. Their nerves became further strained when Gutier Fernández de Toledo, who remained an integral part of Pedro's cortége for over a decade as a decorated military commander, diplomat, and court official, was unwittingly thrust upon the chopping block in 1360. Gutier, who Pedro suspected was fraternizing with the enemy, was ambushed by assassins disguised as negotiators, and beheaded. Before the doomed man was killed, he was allowed to pen one final – and many say prophetic – letter to Pedro: "My Lord...I kiss your hands and take leave of you, now to journey before an even greater lord than yourself...At the moment of my death, I give you my final counsel – if you do not put aside the dagger, if you do not stop committing such murders, then you shall lose your realm and place your person in the greatest jeopardy..."

Pedro took no heed of Gutier's wise words and ordered the deaths of foes and friends alike with the kind of casual indifference one maintains when ordering lunch. Likewise, this extended to Pedro's callous and disrespectful treatment of his victims' bodies. Castilian noble Garcilaso de la Vega II was another who inadvertently wandered into his execution in 1351. His headless body was then tossed out of the Alcázar's tallest tower and into the street, where it was trampled upon by a stampede of bulls. Infante Juan of Aragón, who like the others was deceived into parting with his weapons, met a similar fate. The prince's cold corpse was also tossed out of the window, and the remnants later dumped in the River Guadalquivir.

Such morbidly riveting tales only scratch the surface when it comes to the colorful tapestry of history that has unfolded, and continues to unfold, in the Alcázar. In the same breath, Pedro is only one of the fascinating characters who inhabited these fabled grounds, which many deem the most dazzling "jewel in Seville's crown." But this paradisaical complex of enchanting palaces and gardens is far more than just an impressive landmark – it is evidence of the beauty birthed from the multicultural Andalusian timeline, a harmonious masterpiece crafted by Muslims, Christians, and Jews.

The royal estate, with 17,000 square meters of spectacular structures and 7 hectares of lavish gardens, is even more sublime in the nighttime. The rambling Moorish arches, and the gorgeous detail of the fairy-tale turrets and curtain walls – from the striking shapes of the rectangular merlons, capped with triangular cones, to the coarse, aged texture and smears of damp discoloring the ancient facade – are all the more emphasized by the torches dotted throughout the premises. But following the departure of the nocturnal visitors, the interactive tour guides (clad in elaborate costumes of historical figures just hours before), and the last of the staff, the Alcázar, some say, becomes an intoxicating, sinister maze almost impossible to escape.

The Alhambra and the Alcázar of Seville: The History of the Famous Fortresses Constructed by the Moors in Spain offers a virtual tour of the fortress palaces, and it chronicles their history and legacy, including the events that inspired, advanced, and stalled their development throughout the years. Along with pictures of important people, places, and events, you will learn about the Alhambra and the Alcázar of Seville like never before.

The Alhambra and the Alcázar of Seville: The History of the Famous Fortresses Constructed by the Moors in Spain

The Dawn of Moorish Spain

"My God, how beautiful it is when hold by the right hand of the incomparable king...Rejoice at Ismail, thanks to whom God has honored you and made you happy. May the Islam subsist thanks to him so strongly, that it will be the defense of the throne!" – translated from poem found in the northern portico of Generalife

Before diving into the legend of Alhambra, it's necessary to understand the place's origins, and to tell its story, the hands of time must be turned back 4,000 years. Unsurprisingly, much of the city's early history is highly speculative, and thus it can only be outlined through the meager clues that have been left behind. Even today, a lot is left to the imagination of the city's successors.

One of these theories found an origin tale in the Christian Bible, suggesting that the city had been named after Grana, the daughter of Noah. Another version intimated that Granada, which was previously known as Iliberia, was founded by the great-great-granddaughter of Hercules, Liberia. Others claimed that Iberus, grandson of Tubal, had erected the city and christened it "Granata," naming it after Nata, the daughter of Liberia.

Most of these theories have since been put to bed as myths by modern historians, and with the aid of ancient records and findings recovered from excavation sites, a more or less accurate timeline has since been generated.

Humbly sized Iberian tribes called the "Turdulos," said to be the most civilized of all the inhabitants in the region at the time, made their homes in Granada since as early as 2000-1500 BCE. They cultivated and bred communities on the land bordering what would one day become the colorful, thriving city. To the Turdulos, however, home was Ihverir. In this growing city, the Turdulos lived alongside the Phoenicians, their neighbors' small colonies scattered along the coastline.

In 550 BCE, the decades' worth of peace and harmony in Ihverir was disrupted by the unforeseen invasion of the Carthaginians, who hailed from the ancient city of Tunis in Northern Africa. The reins of power were soon prised out of the Phoenicians' grasps, and fell snugly into the palms of the Carthaginians. A blended city known as Elybirge would soon arise from the ashes.

Approximately 3 centuries later, the Romans descended upon Elybirge, and once again, control of the city switched hands. The Romans transformed the town into a municipality, placing it under authority of a local government. The city was re-branded in Latin as "*Florentia,*" meaning "city full of flowers or fruits." Understandably so, this intriguing city, covered with lush meadows, handsome forests, glistening greenery, and sensational scenery, was one that everyone had their eye on.

While Iliberis was under Roman rule, the lack of attention and security designated to the city made it easy for those watching on the sidelines to swoop in when the city was at its most vulnerable. The breaking point came in the 5th century CE, and during the slow but definitive crumble of the Roman Empire, it would not be long before the Visigoths sniffed out a new opportunity. The Visigoths, a term used to describe nomadic Germanic tribes, had a poor reputation among the Greeks and Romans. They were scorned as uncouth "barbarians," and were condemned for being "different" and "unsophisticated." Be that as it may, the Romans appeared to have no qualms when it came to allying with the Visigoths. It was said that the ensuing Gothic invasion of Spain, France, and Italy had been orchestrated by the Romans, a last-ditch attempt by an empire wobbling on its last legs.

The takeover of the Iberian Peninsula – the second largest peninsula in the continent, encompassing most of Portugal, Spain, Andorra, and a slim slice of France – was not a single operation but instead required efforts by the Roman-sponsored migrations of the Sueves, Alani, Vandals, Visigoths, and other tribes. The Visigoths first set foot on the peninsula in the year 416, where they were tasked with forcefully re-instituting Roman authority upon other Germanic invaders who had occupied the land. Initially, the Visigoths followed instructions to a tee, but as time progressed, it appeared that there may have been reason to have been suspicious of the Visigoths after all. In 418, they were relocated to France, where they established a makeshift kingdom of their own in Toulouse. When they inevitably wisened up to their employer's increasingly fragile authority, they realized it would not take much to squeeze the disintegrating empire out of the picture.

In 429, as the Vandals retired to Africa, the Visigoths poured back into Spain and claimed the land. Artifacts and records that have survived from the Visigoth (or as historians call it, "Invisigoth") period that would have shed light on the accurate statistics of the population under their rule are extremely limited. Not much can be surmised from the smattering of coins, medals, gold, and silver left behind during this mysterious period.

Though their actual contributions cannot be ascertained, a few conclusions have since been drawn. As opposed to the Vandals, the Visigoths were thought to have been more effective rulers, as the town rapidly flourished in size and populace. For the first time, Granada became home to a military base. Meanwhile, the trend of Christianity had also begun to spread its wings. The Visigoths' strengthening of their military has led many to believe that Granada had served as a capital for the province, even back then. Around the same time, a small colony of Jews would also immigrate into the corner of the city and claim that nook as their own, named "Garnata al-yahut."

In the Visigothic empire, the king was elected by "aristocratic peers" as the "chief" of the people. Not only did he defend the interests of his subjects, he served as the general of war. To unify the religion in the kingdom, the law that allowed intermarriage between Visigoths and

Hispano-Romans was repealed, as they hoped to consolidate the city in Arianism. Arianism was a Visigothic rendition of Christianity, one that saw Christ as a great prophet, but disregarded the belief of the Holy Trinity. This period of Arianism did not last long, and following Visigothic leaders soon declared Catholicism the official religion of the kingdom.

The Visigoths remained in power well into the early years of the 8th century, but many attempted to wrestle the area away from them. All of these attempts would eventually fizzle out, with one important exception. Like the city's origin story, what transpired occurred in a time when the art of transcribing and proper document preservation was still in its most primitive stages, so what it was that truly happened forms a hazy picture at best. In addition, these accounts were written by sources from conflicting backgrounds, meaning some details are prone to exaggeration or minimization, on account of bias.

The Muslim or Umayyad Conquest of the Iberian Peninsula was first mentioned in a Christian source, the *Chronicle of 754*, penned that same year. While the book's contents were vague, it made references to a conquest that was characterized by "expressions of horror and grief." Somewhat paradoxically, the same account also painted the same invaders-turned-governors as "legitimate rulers."

The majority of the theories behind what had incited the seemingly impromptu conquest has revolved around 4 different scenarios. The first theory asserts that the attack was designed simply to test the strength of the Visigothic forces. Another theorizes that the African forces had been dispatched to aid a certain side in the civil war at the time, as their efforts would help build a sound bridge for future alliances and conquests. Others claimed it would have been the first in a string of attacks, prompted by a premeditated invasion to enlarge the Muslim territory. Others believed it was purely an invasion of an exceptionally larger nature, but was one that was unplanned or unmotivated by any "strategic intentions."

A more disturbing cause of attack was found in the 9th century account of the Egyptian Muslim historian, Ibn' Abd al-Hakam. In this account, Julian, the Count of Ceuta and a Christian ruler based in North Africa, approached Tariq ibn Ziyad, the Arab ruler of Morocco, with a stunning proposition. Julian, at this instant a hurting father shaking with unimaginable fury, had supposedly appealed to Ziyad for his assistance in the conquest. Julian accused King Roderic, the tyrannical Visigothic ruler of Spain who had only recently risen to the throne in the year 710, of a heinous crime. Apparently, Roderic, who had been successful in ejecting the previous King Witizza from his throne in a ferocious coup, was not just a ruthless and power-hungry dictator but a sexual predator. Roderic had apparently raped Julian's daughter, and her father, now seeking revenge, wanted nothing more than to "send the Arabs against him."

The same account, the authenticity of which remains in dispute to this day, illustrated how Julian had provided the ships, weapons, and all the necessary equipment to bring the Muslims overseas.

Other accounts suggested that the Jews had played an integral role in the conquest, helping to open the gates and allowing their alleged Muslim collaborators and "liberators" easy entry. Even more compelling, some theorists added that the Jewish people seemed to have no trouble adjusting to life under the new Muslim invaders.

In the year 711, the young and bright-eyed General Ziyad arrived with his massive army of 7,000-10,000 troops. They stepped off their ships and set foot upon what is now known as Gibraltar. This was located on the southern tip of the peninsula, its name derived from its previous moniker, *Jabal At-Tariq*, meaning "Rock of Tariq." Despite the hulking size of Ziyad's forces, his troops set off no alarm bells, as vessels of that size cruising through the straits was a relatively common sight.

Ziyad's army was essentially composed of Arab and Berber soldiers, the latter of which spoke a blend of Afro-Asiatic languages and mostly belonged to the Sunni Muslim faith. As the army sprung forth with their surprise ambush, the defensive troops scrambled into position. This may have been foreign territory, but Ziyad and his men bulldozed right through the city, as the defenses, who had been caught off guard, struggled to stave them off. On the 25th of July in 712, these rumbling conflicts would come to a head in an event now known as the "Battle of Guadalete."

Chroniclers closest to the time period seemed to be in agreement that the number of Roderic's troops had dwarfed Ziyad's. One account even claimed that Roderic had up to 100,000 men in his arsenal, but modern historians have placed the figure closer to 33,000. The defending Visigoth army was split in 2 classes. The first was the noble cavalry, which was well outfitted with sturdy mail armor and glinting weapons that included freshly sharpened swords, axes, lances, and maces that they swung over their heads as they charged forward on horseback. The other class, the Visigoth footmen, made up close to 80% of the army. These were typically the poorer folk of the city, and while they had received adequate training, they lacked sufficient armor and wielded second-rate weapons such as spears, clubs, slings, bows and arrows, and other crude weapons of the like that would be no match to those of Ziyad's men.

Regardless of their numbers, the Visigothic forces were in over their heads, as most of the soldiers' first-hand experience on the field was grossly lacking. The morning of the battle, Ziyad breathed new life into his army with an invigorating speech. Ziyad, who was brimming with confidence, assured them that victory was close at hand. He told his men not to be intimidated by death – if the Grim Reaper should take them, the sooner they would earn the fruits of their rewards in the afterlife. He vowed to fight right alongside them, and promised to have the vicious king Roderic's head.

With adrenaline surging in their systems and Ziyad's words ringing in their ears, the Muslim forces kicked off the final stand. They fended off the Visigothic troops all through mid-morning and soon cast them out with missile fire. Ziyad's winning streak would remain uninterrupted throughout the rest of the day, which resulted in the seriously impaired Visigothic forces backpedaling and regrouping numerous times throughout the battle. Ultimately, as the defensive forces steadily weakened, Ziyad's men managed to surround the Gothic headquarters. It was there, as Ziyad had promised, that he rode into the isolated palace and headed straight for Roderic. The pair faced off in a lengthy scuffle until Ziyad whacked the side of Roderic's helmeted head with his trusty scimitar, sending the Visigothic king flying off his luxurious ruby-studded saddle. Roderic's body crumpled to the ground, disappearing into the chaotic sea of hooves, never to be seen again. An overwhelming number of the Visigothic elite were also said to have been slaughtered by Ziyad's men.

A depiction of Berber cavalry overwhelming the Visigoths during the battle

Left without a leader, what remained of the Visigoths quickly surrendered and skedaddled, seeking refuge in Écija, close to Seville. The Muslims rejoiced in the streets and soon replenished Roderic's throne; from then on, they dominated the Iberian Peninsula, which the new leaders renamed "Al-Andalus." The kingdom experienced another drastic makeover in the new reign that unfolded – the Andalusian Umayyad Dynasty. In the years that followed, the new dynasty entered what is now known as the "Islamic Golden Age."

It was precisely in this fast-budding climate, fueled by the explosion of ideas and melting pot of cultures, that the iconic Alhambra would come to fruition.

The Red One

"Give him alms, lady, for there is nothing in life as wretched as being blind in Granada." –
Francisco Alarcon de Icaza, Mexican poet

In the years that followed, the Umayyad dynasty expanded its territory from the Atlantic to the
Pyrenees, a series of seasonally snow-capped mountains in Europe that forms a border between
the nations of Spain and France. For a while, the capital of the Umayyad dynasty lay in Kurtuba.
In time, the monumental empire would be divided into 11 realms, which included the Al-
Ubushna, Ishbiliya, kadis, Tarif, Balansiyya, Al-mariyya, Gharnatah, and more. It was in this
rapidly prospering kingdom that the Islamic Golden Age, a brilliant burst of scientific, cultural,
and philosophical advancements, would propel the dynasty forward.

The Islamic Golden Age lasted between the 8th to the mid-13th centuries. The Islamic empire
had found a unique way to put itself on the map, as it fostered a multicultural community
considered way ahead of its time. It was one of the earliest versions of "universal civilization," as
it welcomed a population of "peoples as diverse as the Chinese, the Indians, the people of the
Middle East and Africa, black Africans, and white Europeans." This deliberate mingling of
cultures activated the rise of a new wave of engineers, scholars, poets, philosophers,
geographers, merchants, and other great thinkers. By incorporating ingredients from their North
African tradition and merging it with the multifaceted cultures of their newly claimed territory,
Moorish Spain was able to make fantastic leaps of advancements in an array of fields such as
agriculture, arts, sciences, navigation, philosophy, technology, and more. It soon carved itself a
name in the Muslim world as the leading hub for science, education, and business.

One of the most significant and life-changing contributions produced during this period was
the pivotal invention of paper. Before then, this sacred recipe was one only the Chinese were
privy to, but Muslim authorities were able to extract the intel from war prisoners after the Battle
of Talas in 751. The Moors upgraded the invention by altering the recipe to suit their needs,
substituting starch in place of the mulberry bark often used by the Chinese. This was helpful
because the Moors preferred the use of pens, whereas the Chinese opted for brushes.

The sudden explosion of knowledge, as well as new and improved creations, would eventually
find its way to Baghdad and Samarkand. By the year 900, hundreds of public libraries and shops
packed with scribes and book-binders had popped up all over Baghdad. It was in this city that the
continuously developing knowledge, along with the craft of paper-making, made its way across
the seas and into the Moorish kingdom of Spain.

The Spanish-based Moors rolled up their sleeves and went to work immediately, playing an
instrumental role of their own in the golden age generated contributions. In the 9th century,

inventor Abbas ibn Firnas engineered one of the world's first flying contraptions, centuries before Da Vinci would put pen to paper with his. Firnas' contraption, which was basically a bizarre mechanism with wings and was somewhat reminiscent of a bird costume, though sure to raise some eyebrows today, was applauded by his peers during the time. To the cheers and hollers of the captivated crowd below him, Firnas succeeded in taking off and soaring for a few satisfying seconds before plummeting straight to the ground, partially fracturing his back.

Another notable invention from Moorish Spain during this precious period was the bridge mill, a water mill component of a bridge structure. They would also impart their flavor onto musical instruments – the modern guitar is said to have been inspired by the Arabic *"oud"* instrument, which was later introduced in Medieval Spain as the *"guitarra moresca,"* or in English, the "Moorish guitar." More evidence of the combined cultures can be found in art, literature, and architecture published during the time.

Among the greatest minds that took to the spotlight in Moorish Spain was Abu Zakariya al-Awwam Ishibili, who pioneered a grafting procedure that would prove pivotal in the surgical world and made waves in the world of botany by singlehandedly naming 500 different species of plants. Another celebrated scholar during this period was Pedro Alfonzo, a Spanish Muslim scientist with a passion for astronomy. Alfonzo had aided in the research of the fledgling science, which he then promoted in the Latin education system. As word of the numerous scientific advancements and triumphs in this region leaked beyond the Al-Andalusian borders, scientists and scholars from across the continent teemed into the kingdom for a dip in the refreshing pool of novel knowledge.

The Moors would also help revitalize the ailing Spanish economy. They founded the silk industry in Al-Andalus and solidified Spain as the center of silk production. The Moors would also dabble in the production of a range of other materials and goods such as cotton, satin, fur, pepper, paper, soaps, maps, and clocks. Under Moorish authority, new libraries, colleges, and public baths were also constructed for the people.

The Moorish presence in Spain has also been praised for the peace and stability brought about by the Umayyad dynasty, Amir Abd al-Rahman I, which lasted roughly between the years of 756 to 1031. It was Amir who had established the Emirate of Cordoba, which was among the most prestigious of the European territories ruled by a dynastic Islamic monarch. It was also said that Amir had been key in unifying the Muslim leaders strewn across Islamic Europe and convincing them into marrying their powers into one, thereby ruling as a single entity.

Amir Abd al-Rahman I

According to ancient chroniclers, the Muslims, Christians, and Jews in Moorish Spain lived in a society that promoted harmony through religious tolerance. While modern historians agree that some form of tolerance and acceptance was indeed exerted, what had been practiced was in fact an antiquated view of equality. Historian Bernard Lewis best sums up the social status of the non-Muslims in an excerpt from his book, *The Jews of Islam:* "Second class citizenship, though second class, is a kind of citizenship. It involves some rights, though not all...[It is] a recognized status, albeit one of inferiority to the dominant group, which is established by law, recognized by tradition, and confirmed by popular assent, is not to be despised." Generally speaking, non-Muslims of Moorish Spain experienced freedom to a certain extent, so long as they adhered to a special set of rules. While these restrictions and regulations may seem inconceivable today, the non-Muslims were far better off than other prisoners and conquered people of their time. Unlike others who had been browbeaten by abrupt changes in management, the non-Muslims and pagans were not enslaved, nor were they shunned to live in sleazy ghettos. They were not required to convert, nor were they punished, penalized, or executed for their beliefs. They were welcomed in almost every profession, and could contribute as they pleased to the burgeoning culture. While this was the case, most of the non-Muslims pursued less desirable means of income, such as working in butcheries and tanning, but there were also those who chose to work in banking and money-handling.

To identify the non-Muslims and pagans of the area, otherwise known as *"dhimmi"* and *"majus,"* respectively, authorities ensured they sported badges pinned to their chests or sleeves. Construction of new non-Muslim places of worship were either ceased or curbed. *Dhimmi* and *majus* were prohibited from carrying weapons, bequeathing or inheriting any property from Muslims, and employing Muslim slaves. The average non-Muslim or pagan could not appear, provide evidence, or testify in a court of law, and were awarded less compensation for injuries and other matters of the like than their non-dhimmi counterparts. The restrictions even touched on marriage laws; while non-Muslim men were forbidden from tying the knot with Muslim women, a Muslim was free to exchange vows with *dhimmi* or *majus* women if they so wished.

Apart from the rules mentioned above, the *dhimmi* and *majus* were left to their own devices under the following stipulations. First, they were to concede to and fully acknowledge Islamic authority, embracing the superiority of their new leaders. In exchange for their freedom to worship, they, too, were required to remain respectful of the Muslim faith, as well as other religions. They were not to speak ill of any other religion, particularly Islam, and were expected to stay within the boundaries of their own religious circles. Any attempt at conversion to any faith but Islam was entirely out of the question. Finally, they were commanded to cough up a special tax known as the *"jizya"* to Muslim authorities. They were not exempt from any other taxes, and were usually slapped with higher fees and interest rates.

The *dhimmi* and *majus* were not pleased with but could easily make do with these demands. Gradually, they began to indulge themselves with the foreign Muslim culture, and vice versa. Christians who voluntarily learned Arabic, took on Arabic names for themselves, and espoused certain styles of Muslim clothing and customs were referred to as *"Mozarabs."*

Unfortunately, not all of the Moorish rulers were as tolerant. Having risen to the so-called "de facto" throne of Al-Andalus between the late 10th and early 11th centuries, Sultan Almanzor expressed a much more overt contempt for the *dhimmi*. Shortly into his reign, he ordered the looting, torching, and destruction of several of the *dhimmi* churches, and he later tightened the already strict regulations in hopes of further oppressing the non-believers. Christians, in particular, were especially despised by the new Muslim authorities. The new restrictions imposed upon them seemed downright petty. They were no longer allowed to build or live in houses taller than their Muslim neighbors. In the streets, they were required by law to shuffle out of the way for any Muslim that comes across their path. Worse yet, Christians and Jews were barred from displaying any signs of their faith in public. Just the plain act of being spotted with a bible could mean a severe penalty, or even execution.

The animosity against non-Muslims only intensified from there, and the tension came to a head when carnage erupted in the form of a pogrom on December 30, 1066. The Jewish residents of Granada, Spain, fell target to an unanticipated onslaught from a furious Muslim mob. The attackers went on to butcher up to 4,000 of the Jewish inhabitants. Not long after the massacre, the mob captured Joseph Ibn Naghrela, a Jewish vizier who was a high-ranking court official for the Andalusian king. Naghrela flailed, thrashed, and screamed for help, but eventually he was crucified at the hands of his kidnappers.

The mass murder of the Jewish people seemed to have been one of the major contributors to the Moors' dwindling power and authority. As soon as the Christian leaders spotted the multiplying chinks in the Moorish armor, they embarked on a highly productive quest to take back what they deemed was theirs. The first Muslim stronghold in Toledo collapsed in 1085, triggering a domino effect of great magnitude. In the span of just a few years, 9 of the flags on Muslim territories in Spain and Portugal were uprooted, and Christian flags replaced them. The 2 territories that remained under Muslim authority were the Tarif and the Al-Mariyya.

The recaptured Muslim territories underwent yet another name change. Al-Ubushna became "Lisboa," and Ishbiliya became "Sevilla." Balansiyya was now "Valencia," and Kadis was Cádiz. Kurtuba reverted to "Cordoba," and Gharnata became "Granada." With these territories now back in Christian hands, the remaining Muslim inhabitants were downgraded to second class citizens. They now faced many of the same restrictions they had imposed upon the Christians just months before.

It would be Muhammad ibn Yusuf ibn Nasr, a descendant of the Prophet Muhammad's comrades-in-arms, who decided that it was time for Muslims to dig their heels into the ground. On April 18, 1232, he declared himself Muhammad I, the great Sultan of Arjona. In the years that followed, he proclaimed ownership of the Guadix, Baza, and Jaen territories. Come May, 5 years later, Muhammad, along with a band of meticulously selected and reinforced troops, marched into the city of Granada. There, he named himself sultan, planting the seeds of the Nasrid Dynasty.

A contemporary depiction of Muhammad I

Rather than grapple with the Christian forces stationed there, the new sultan chose to join forces with his opponents. The sultan allowed Granada to become the vassal, or subordinate, state of Ferdinand III, the Christian king of Castile. Historians believe that this level-headed approach was why Muhammad had been the choice candidate for the dynamic dynasty, one that would reign for the next 250 years.

A Ruby Arising from Blood

"...I hear voices crying, 'Yield! That is true wisdom!'

But I reply, 'Poison would be a sweeter draught to me

Than such a cup of shame!'

...the barbarians wrest me from my realm,

And my soldiers forsake me...

When I fell upon the foe...

Hoping for death, I flung myself into the fray;

But alas, my hour had not yet come!" - Mutamid Ibn Abbad, the Poet-King of Seville, upon losing the Alcázar

In order to fully appreciate the wonder that is the Alcázar, it's necessary to understand the history of Seville and the events leading up to its creation.

Seville has most likely been occupied since the Neolithic Era by enterprising people who wished to capitalize on the fertile land and the Guadalquivir, the second-longest river in all of Spain. In the 1st century BCE, Seville, a river port and bridge between Andalusia and the Atlantic, was transformed into a bustling commercial crossroads between the North-East and Western Iberian territories by the Romans. The Roman settlers proceeded to rule the land now known as Seville for more than 600 years.

The first Roman colony in the area, which was christened "Italica" by its founders, lay about 6 miles from modern-day Seville. Under its competent conquerors, Italica swiftly evolved into a vibrant metropolis serviced by aqueducts, a 25,000-seater amphitheater, and iconic Romanesque structures. It was in this luxurious locale that the future Roman emperors Trajan and Hadrian were born.

An ancient bust of Trajan

A bust of Hadrian in Venice

In 49 BCE, Italica was renamed "Hispalis" by Julius Caesar, and it continued to expand under Caeasar and his successors, in time encompassing a significant portion of what is now Seville today.

The plot that would one day become the Alcázar, situated close to the literal heart of Seville, was turned into the grounds of the Collegium, or College of Olearians, in the 1st century CE. *Collegia*, as defined by William Smith in *The Dictionary of Greek & Roman Antiquities*, were "civic, religious, or fraternal associations." Whether the Collegium of Olearians served specifically as a guild for businessmen, a burial society, or a social club, is uncertain; one can only assume that the association was equipped with a governing body modeled after the Senate of Rome, and that the club boasted a *curia*, or a meeting hall.

Not much, if anything, is known about the Roman establishment's appearance, but excavations conducted in recent years have given archaeologists a glimpse of its décor, as well as the construction materials the Romans might have utilized. The green hues found on 30 fragments of Romanesque wall paintings lifted from the excavation site of the Patio de Banderas, for instance, is believed to be a mix of celadonite and chlorite. "Refractive materials," such as crushed glass, and light-refracting minerals were used to create shades of Egyptian-blue.

In the early years of the 5th century CE, Seville was seized by a Central European tribe known as the "Silingi Vandals" from Silesia, but their dominion over Seville was short-lived, for they were quickly ousted and replaced by the nomadic Germanic tribespeople otherwise known as the Visigoths in the year 461 CE. The Visigoths swept away the ruins of the *collegium*, not wanting this valuable plot of land to go to waste, and in its stead, erected a basilica dedicated to deacon-turned-saint Vincent of Saragossa, a native of Huesca and the first martyr of Spain. There appears to be no surviving sketches or descriptions of this particular church, but it is safe to assume that it shared many of the characteristics of other Visigothic churches in Spain at the time.

It would be reasonable to assume that like Spain's oldest church, raised by Visigothic King Recceswinth in the 7th century CE in honor of San Juan de Banos, the St. Vincent Basilica in Seville was fashioned out of dry ashlar stone blocks, and consisted of 3 aisles, "latticed windows" chiseled out of stone, and walls frescoed with decorative, rather than religiously symbolic imagery. The basilica's arches would have most likely been somewhat shaped like a horseshoe, a distinctive architectural feature that were supposedly the creation of either the Visigoths or 3rd century Syrians. These so-called "horseshoe arches" became associated with Muslims in Iberia later on, for it was the Moors who popularized the design and incorporated it into many of their structures. Visitors with a trained eye can still spot the Visigothic shafts and capitals still used in the Palace of Peter of Castile (Pedro the Cruel) today.

It was reportedly in the St. Vincent Basilica that the Visigoths buried Saint Isidore of Seville, who was, as the Spanish council of bishops who canonized him in 653 called him, "an illustrious teacher of our time and the glory of the Catholic Church." This pious figure also authored the *Etymologiae*, the first comprehensive encyclopedia written from a Catholic point of view. Here, Isidore's sacred body lay in a handsome stone tomb until the basilica was dismantled, after which his body was then relocated to a church in Leon. The tombstone of Honorato, Bishop of Seville, may have also been housed in the St. Vincent Basilica for some time, but it was later transferred to the Seville Cathedral.

Seville slipped into the hands of the Moors in the year 712, and chroniclers attribute this consequential turn of events to the insatiable sexual appetite of Rodrigo, the last king of the Spanish Visigoths. In 711, Rodrigo kidnapped, raped, and fell in love with a young woman by the name of Florinda, who was taking a dip in the Rio Tajo when he chanced upon her. The highly abusive and toxic qualities to their "relationship" aside, Florinda, as it turns out, was none other than the youngest daughter of Rodrigo's comrade, Count Julian. Outraged by Rodrigo's betrayal, Julian partnered with the Moorish Emir Muda bin Nusayr and concocted a plan to take Spain for themselves. In the autumn of 711, General Tariq ibn Ziyan and a fleet of war vessels containing an army of 9,000 strong ventured out from the North African coast and forged across the azure waters of the Gibraltar Strait. Weeks later, the Moorish soldiers reached the coast of southern Spain and descended upon the foreign land. The Moors, evidently, were here to stay, and their raids eventually reached as far as the Pyrenees. For the next 5 centuries, the Moors presided over a substantial amount of Spanish terrain, their customs and art inevitably bleeding into the local culture.

Emir Muda bin Nusayr was resolved to make his intentions of permanent residency known to his new subjects. For starters, the metropolis of Hispalis was rebranded "Ixbilia," and the Betis River renamed the "Guad el Kevir." The names "Ixbilia" and "Guad el Kevir" became so tightly tied to the locals' identity that future generations opted to retain the Moorish roots of both names. Not long after, the emir ordered the destruction of St. Vincent's Basilica in Seville. Massive squares of vegetation, gravel, and fauna surrounding the defunct basilica were also cleared to make room for the new fortress and palace that would be constructed in its place. The Moors named this new complex the "Real Alcázar (Royal Alcázar)," derived from the Arabic word "*al-qasr,*" meaning "fortress," and its synonym, "*castillo,*" meaning "castle." The Alcázar, as demanded by the emir, was to be mighty enough to withstand all attacks from Vikings, vengeful Visigoths, and other potential enemies.

In the year 913, the Caliph of Cordoba, Abdurrahman III an-Nasir, commissioned the construction of a network of new government buildings. The Dar al-lmara, as the caliph called it, was to be built in the south of the city, furnished with defensive walls that encircled the Old Town of Seville, including the original Alcázar facilities and the old Roman walls. Though these Moorish walls were partially toppled by the Glorious Revolution of 1868, some sections, such as those wrapped around the Alcázar, still stand today. The Dar al-lmara, plainly put, was the core of the now-existing Royal Alcázar.

It was under the guidance of Caliph an-Nasir that a full-fledged "palatial fortress" began to materialize. Long before the layout of the Alcázar became the free-form, multifaceted arrangement that it is today, reminiscent of a medieval castle in itself from an aerial perspective, it began as a quadrangular plot of land enclosed by stone walls sealed with mud mortar. Alas, no known remnants of the Dar al-lmara or other features of the Alcázar from this period exist.

As per the disintegration of the Caliphate in 1031, Seville was converted into a "*taifa* kingdom." Al-Andalus, or the territories of Islamic Iberia, were splintered into several *taifas*, or "princely states." The Abbadid Dynasty, headed by patriarch and former *qadi* (magistrate of a Shari'a court) of Seville, Abu al-Qasim Muhammad ibn Abbad, soon surpassed, then absorbed competing Muslim caliphates, such as the Zayrids, the Hammudids, and the Amirids, amongst others, until it reigned supreme. Through al-Qasim's leadership, as well as the city's strategic proximity to the Guadalquivir and its commercial relationship with North African and

Mediterranean merchants, Seville soon dominated as the most economically, politically, and resourcefully prosperous of all the *taifas*.

The Abbadid emirs made good use of the state's tremendous wealth and continued to build upon the Alcázar, in particular expanding westward. Al-Qasim's son and heir, Emir Abbad II al-Mu'tadid, who directed much of the westward expansion, also gave the new wing its name; he called it the "Qasr al-Mubarak," otherwise known as the "Palace of Good Fortune," or the "Blessed Place" for short.

Those who ruled after Abbad II continued to improve upon the Qasr al-Mubarak with regular refurbishments and artistic additions that aligned with their faith, namely, the use of elaborate geometric patterns, from perplex figures resembling multi-pointed stars and snowflakes to overlapping shapes; elegant calligraphy etched into walls; and arabesque aesthetics, an artistic style defined by floral patterns, spirals, and a balance between symmetry and nature.

It is important to note the lack of animal and human representation in the décor of the Alcázar during this time, since doing so was against the Quran. Instead, Moorish artists focused on art born from mathematics, as this scientific field was to them a means of expression that brought them closer to Allah. The geometric art left behind by the Moorish chapter of the Alcázar is undoubtedly stunning, but it is even more extraordinary when one considers that these shapes and patterns were designed with nothing but a ruler, a pair of compasses, and the artist's rich imagination.

The sumptuous selection of handmade arabesque tiles painstakingly glued onto the lofty walls, vaulted ceilings, and floors of the Abbadid palace is another unique Moorish trait. The brilliant patterns of the wall and ceiling tiles came in swatches of lapiz-blue, greens, and other cool colors. The faded glazed tiles now seen delicately laid over the gardens and walls of the Moorish palace within the Alcázar, however, are not the original pieces. While it was the Iberian Muslims who popularized the use of "patterned walls and floor tiles," the craft was first perfected by Moorish rulers in early Persia. Given the strict rules of the "Islamic Code of Non-Representation," Muslim artists had to devise a way to enliven a room and captivate the room's owners with nothing but repetitive, yet mesmerizing abstract shapes and patterns.

To add to the mystique, exactly how the Moorish artists were able to carve the intricate swirls and floral accents that bordered the tall arches and garnished the vaulted ceilings is still a matter of dispute. Most assume that wooden scaffolding similar to the ones used by ancient Egyptian laborers was most likely used, but a few insist that such scaffolding would have never been limber enough to support the artists when confronted by tricky angles and hard-to-reach corners.

Either way, the designs and work of the Moorish artists, craftsmen, and laborers were so timelessly alluring that many of the original elements, such as the arches, tiles, and arabesque styles, were preserved, augmented, or enriched by future residents. The Moorish flavors were particularly embraced by sovereigns who ushered the Alcázar through its Gothic and Mudejar phases. A tribute to Emir Muhammad al-Mu'tamid Ibn Abbad, son of Abbad II and grandson of al-Qasim, the "Poet King of Sevilla" and the last of the Abbadid *taifa* rulers, stands in the Alcázar's *Jardin de la Galera* (Garden of the Galley) to this day.

Al-Mu'tamid was only 13 when he inherited the title of emir and the dominion of southern Spain, including Seville, in 1069. 13th century Shafi'i Islamic biographer Ibn Khallikan described the cultured king as such: "[He] was gifted with a handsome face, a body perfect in its proportions, a colossal stature, a liberal hand, penetration of intellect, presence of mind, and a just perception. By these qualities he surpassed all his contemporaries; and moreover before ambition led him to aspire after power, he had looked into literature with a close glance and an acute apprehension; so that by his quick intelligence, he acquired an abundant stock of information...With these accomplishments, [al-Mu'tamid] derived from his genius the talent of expressing his thoughts in an ornate style. He composed also pieces of verse remarkable for sweetness...expressing perfectly well what he wished to say, and displaying such excellence as caused them to be copied by literary men..."

With al-Mu'tamid in power, Seville, and in turn the Alcázar, became the principal learning center of Muslim Iberia. The emir kitted out the libraries of the Alcázar with hundreds of manuscripts in educational and fictional genres alike, and hosted routine literary meetings. He also had something of an obsession with "*majalis al-uns*," or "carefree gatherings," attended by local wordsmiths, poets, scholars, and entertainers on a weekly basis. Regulars at these literary soirées could expect lyrical battles, live music, and endless booze.

The lute-playing Al-Mu'tamid was beloved by his subjects not only for his unparalleled way with words, but for his dedication to advancing education and protecting the rights and talents of his creative and learned subjects. Whereas Emir Abbad II was notorious for his despotism and his unsparing attitude towards his subjects, his son was a fair and liberal-minded ruler who effortlessly attracted respected writers and respectable scholars to his court in the Alcázar. His court, as Khallikan put it, was a "haling place of travelers, the rendezvous of poets, the point to which all hopes were directed and the haunt of men of talent."

As emir, Al-Mu'tamid went on to capture and claim hold of Cordoba, the kingdom of Murcia on the Costa Calida, and the Andalusian city of Jaen, among other territories. For over two decades, the emir reigned undisturbed, until King Alfonso VI of Leon and Castile raided and secured Toledo, another "chief center of Muslim scholarship," in 1085. When Al-Mu'tamid refused to shell out the tributes demanded by Alfonso, the merciless Castilian monarch dispatched his soldiers to the emir's most prized city, Seville, and laid siege to its fortress. Al-Mu'tamid stubbornly tried to hold out, but the Christian forces were far more advanced, not to mention far stronger than anticipated. It pained him to do so, but he eventually had to appeal to the sultan of the North African Almoravids, Yūsuf ibn Tāshufīn, for aid. Yūsuf, who had just recently acquired the entirety of Morocco and its military forces, quickly agreed, and in 1090, sent a legion of his "veiled warriors" to chase the Castilian and Aragonese forces out of southern Spain.

Much to the chagrin of Emir al-Mu'tamid, the resilience and opulence of the Alcázar was not lost on Yūsuf. Thus, the latter began a campaign to dethrone the former, and he eventually seized Seville and its fortress for himself. The disgraced emir was then exiled to Morocco, where he remained a prisoner in body and mind until his death.

The tribute in the Garden of the Galley is a plain, but tasteful stone column established as a way to immortalize the emir's fateful exile. Printed onto one side of the column is his name and the date of his exile – September 7, 1091 – as well as a brief passage that makes mention of his accomplishments as a poet. On the opposite side of the column are a couple of lines from one of the emir's poems, a poignant wish that was never granted to him:

"God grant that I may die in Seville,

And that our graves be opened there at the resurrection."

José Luiz Bernardes Ribeiro's picture of the Column of al-Mu'tamid

As instructed by Yūsuf and his Berber inheritors, the governmental sector of the Alcázar was temporarily suspended, for the capital of the Almoravids remained in Marrakesh. That said, Almoravid architects were ordered to further extend the palace to the banks of the Guadalquivir.

At first, the Almoravids accused the Iberian Muslims of straying from the Quran, and condemned the luxury openly exhibited by the affluent Sevillean Moors. The new government enforced rigid regulations regarding architectural styles and art forms allowed in their communities, permitting only basic shapes, rudimentary palettes, and traditional geometric patterns, which were reflected in their additions to the Alcázar. Only during the second half of their fleeting 56-year reign did the Almoravids loosen up the rules, enticed by the tempting magnificence of the Al-Andalus.

The Moorish Alcázar was most likely grander in terms of space and design than in its furnishings. Up until more recent centuries, wooden furniture was a rarity, more so in conventional Islamic societies, the main reason for this being its high cost. Timber was constantly reused, and more often set aside for the building of boats, roofs, shutters, and doors. Most of the Spanish Moors, including the royals, preferred to kneel or sit Lotus-style on plush carpets, "firmly-stuffed bolsters," and soft cushions placed atop raised platforms and projections.

The Moorish craftsmen hired by the Almoravids and other Muslim rulers of the Alcázar treated the expensive resource that was wood accordingly. Every last inch of the humble helpings apportioned to them were utilized by the scrappy artists and transformed into statement art pieces through 3 artistic techniques. First, the *mashrabiyya*, wherein "lathe-turned" wood is woven into "grilled" window screens. The second was geometric marquetry, which calls for covering surfaces with wood veneers carefully laid out side by side to create various patterns. Finally, inlay, which, as its name suggests, involves inlaying, or embedding colored chunks of wood into the crevices punched into larger tablets of wood. The one article of wooden furniture presumably owned by the Moors in Alcázar was the *minbar*, a flowery wooden throne placed atop a set of three short steps.

In early 1147, the Almoravids were ejected from their seat of power when they failed to quash an insurrection raised by Ibn Tumart. The Almoravids contended vigorously for the reins, but they were never able to recover from the bedlam incited by Tumar's revolt. Their lastflickering flame of hope was snuffed out when the Almoravid king, Ishaq ibn Ali, was assassinated in Marrakesh that April by the Almohad Caliphate.

The Almohad Caliphate once again reinstated Seville as the capital of the Al-Andalus, and the Alcázar as its governing headquarters and a place of Islamic learning. Like the previous Moroccan sovereigns, the Almohads aggrandized the metropolis with renovations and expansions to the existing Arabic architecture, concentrating especially on the grand Sevillean fortress, as well as a series of new mosques and seasonal royal residences.

The builders and designers employed by the Almohad rulers were also restricted by the society's belief in religious reformation, but this did nothing to stifle their creativity. The *Mezquita de Sevilla,* or the Grand Mosque of Seville, and the minaret-turned-bell tower, the *Torre Giralda,* are just some of the Almohad artists' magnum opuses. On top of the Almohads' penchant for geometric patterns and ornamental designs, architects and engineers integrated the rectangular arcades, splendid brick and stone facades, interlaced, as well as trademark poly-lobed arches (arches with a series of semi-circles or "lobes" for the intrados) into their plans for the Alcázar.

The Almohads, like many other Arabic rulers and sovereigns from dry nations, had a special fondness for resplendent gardens and springs, so much so that they often constructed their own springs in their palaces. Most significantly, gardens in the Quran were used as meditative spaces, and to symbolize the paradise that awaited those who subscribed to the faith. As such, several gardens were planted within and outside the walls of the Alcázar. One of these miniature vegetative paradises was a deluxe "4-part garden...with deeply sunken quadrants" known as the *"Patio de la Casa de Contratacion"* ("Courtyard of the Hiring House"). It continues to be preserved in the center of the Andalusian public works and finances offices of the modern-day Alcázar.

The courtyard was originally found within one of the buried Moorish palaces in the fortress. Like the *Patio del Crucero* (Courtyard of the Cross), the brick courtyard of the *Casa de Contratacion* was shaped like an even-armed cross, with a lush flowerbed in each quadrant, watered by 4 *acequias*, or narrow irrigation canals placed 2 meters above them. Finally, in the center of the courtyard, there was a babbling, triple-tiered fountain.

The Renaissance-era rulers of the Alcázar who later inherited the gardens elected to keep many of the plants installed by the previous tenants. Excavations during the 1970s revealed traces of centuries-old orange, lemon, and palm trees, as well as myrtle hedges, particularly in the *Huerta de la Alcoba* (Alcove Orchard). The *acequias* are thought to have been connected to the *Estanque de Mercurio* (Mercury Pool) by the Grutesco Gallery, which holds over 670 cubic meters (670,000 liters) of water.

Mihael Grmek's picture of the gardens from Galeria de Grutescos

The most well-known of all the Moorish gardens in Alcázar is the *Patio del Yeso,* or "Courtyard of Stucco"; it is also the oldest surviving segment of the original Alcázar. This *patio,* marked by its rectangular reflective pool, keyhole doors, and the webs of squid-shaped stucco tracery that crowned and filled the gaps of the poly-lobed arches, was easily the most magnificent of the courtyard within the Alcázar at the time. Bearing this in mind, the palace by the *Patio del Yeso* was reserved for the Almohad caliphs Abu Yaqub Yusuf and Abu Yusuf al-Mansur; Pedro the Cruel also lived here as he awaited the completion of his new royal residence. Christian rulers later modernized the *Patio del Yeso* by adding a *qubba,* or a "square reception hall," capped with a wooden ceiling, to the courtyard. The *qubba* remained in use for several centuries until it was retired by its occupants in the 1700s.

To the right of the Maiden's Courtyard was the *Dormitorio de los Reyes Moros*, the Bedroom of the Moorish Kings, or the *Alcoba Real*, the Royal Bedroom. The caliphs slept in this "open bedroom" to escape the sweltering summer heat. The interior was split into two chambers, accessible by an entrance composed of 3 horseshoe arches. The room to the left, the "Lost Steps Room," was outfitted with a coffered ceiling, an archway with 13 lobes, and a passageway that led straight to the patio.

A hypnotic medley of geometric tiles in all shapes and colors, paired with wooden slabs delicately inlaid with colorful tiles coated every inch of the walls and ceilings. Extravagant plaster friezes, along with patriotic medallions of Gothic-style lions were added to the walls by 15th century Catholic monarchs.

In the Alcázar the Almohad caliphs remained until Castilian King Ferdinand III reclaimed Cordoba, Mucia, and Jaen, and besieged Seville in 1247. The Almohads and Sevillean locals put up a bitter fight, hurling projectiles and tipping over buckets of boiling oil through the crenels of the Alcázar walls, and they managed to keep the Castilian invaders at bay for some time, but by the summertime, their resilience began to waver. By then, they were rapidly being picked off by famine, dehydration, and disease. They finally surrendered in November of the following year, and as stipulated by the agreement struck between the Castilian king and Almohad caliph, hundreds of thousands of Spanish Muslims were "escorted" to Granada or North Africa by Christian soldiers. Only Jews and Moriscos, or converted Muslims, were permitted to stay.

On the 22nd of December, 1248, King Ferdinand III, along with 24,000 of his subjects from Castile and Leon, marched into Seville. They were accompanied by a glittering procession, complete with a stately carriage towed by 4 white stallions and an entourage bearing the ivory statue of the "Virgin of the Kings," and beautiful maidens showering the streets with baskets of flowers. Ferdinand was the first Castilian king in 5 centuries to succeed in reclaiming Spain from the Moors.

A contemporary depiction of King Ferdinand III of Castile

Following the Reconquista, which culminated with the "Siege of Seville," Ferdinand moved his court to the Alcázar, where he remained until his death in 1252, closely followed by his canonization as Seville's patron saint. Ferdinand's son, Alfonso X, patterned his governing style after his father's, maintaining a religious tolerance that extended to his Christian, Jewish, and even Muslim subjects alike. It was this thriving, multicultural atmosphere that triggered the next stage of the fortress' development.

A contemporary depiction of Alfonso X

A City Within a City

"How lazily the sun goes down in Granada, it hides beneath the water, it conceals in the Alhambra!" – Ernest Hemingway

In the year 1238, the Nasrids ordered the construction of a new kingdom on the Al-Sabika Hill called "Alhambra," which translates to the "red one" in Arabic. This was a reference to the sultan's ravishing palace, which was to be built with sun-baked tapia, as well as earth and clay-and-gravel bricks colored with a distinctive reddish-brown tint. The new defensive citadel that would be restored and rebuilt was to be called "Alcazaba."

The blueprints of the Alhambra were a sight to behold. These ancient scrolls outlined plans to erect walls that stretched 1.73 miles long, as well as the assembly of 30 new towers in this "city within a city," accessible by 4 gates. The dozens of structures constructed within would be built for 3 primary purposes: a military stronghold and defense system in Alcazaba for amped up security; a *"medina,"* or *"city,"* where court officials could live and work; and finally, an elegant environment and residence fit for the royal family. The miniature city would be connected by winding paths, opulent gardens, and magnificent gates, but barricades and defense systems would also be strategically set in place throughout the city to safeguard the community.

When construction began, the Alcazaba citadel was set to be built in a triangle, as seen from a bird's eye view, upon the foundations of the existing palace's walls. The citadel, which was to be filled with hulking towers and impenetrable borders, would serve as the chief defense base for Alhambra. This would not be the first time that the time-honored "Red One" was used as a fortress. Back in the 9th century, Sawwar ben Hamdum was said to have sought shelter in the castle that would become part of the Alcazaba. Here, he redressed the castle as a fortress and military stronghold.

The Alcazaba, its construction overseen by Muhammed I, is the oldest section of the Alhambra complex. Muhammed later went on to build 3 more towers in the citadel, as well as the bulwarks, or powerful defensive walls, around the new fortress. The original triad of towers consisted the Torre de la Vela, or the "Watchtower;" the Torre Quebrada, the "Broken Tower;" and lastly, the 5-cornered entity that was the Torre del Homenaje, meaning "the Keep." Much later on, a fourth tower, the Torre de la Pólvora, or the "Gunpowder Tower," was added.

A 20th century photo of some of the Alcazaba's ruins

The Torre Quebrada

The Tower of Justice

The Torre de la Vela was the first to be erected of all the citadel towers, and it remains the grandest of these 4 towers. It loomed over the city, the peak of its tower clearly visible from miles away. One of the Vela's exclusive features was its bell tower, its bell said to have been among the largest in the world during the period. This bell was so splendid that a cork forest had to be auctioned off in order for the sultan to obtain the funds needed to purchase the brass beauty. The first bell tower was set up in the corner of the fortress, but it would be moved to different areas in the years that followed – once because it was struck by lightning.

Traditionally, these bells were rung to signal a change in "irrigation turns." Young maidens were also said to have clambered up the tower, as an urban legend dictated that tolling the bell assured a marriage by the end of the same year. Today, 4 flags proudly planted on the roofs of the Vela can be seen flapping in the wind against the halo of the sun: the crimson and yellow Spanish flag; the green and white Andalusian flag; the red and green Granada flag; and one in blue, emblazoned with a ring of white stars, a symbol of the European Union.

The Alcazaba would also serve as the living quarters for the sultan's military officials and soldiers. A walkway segregated the Alcazaban community. One side was populated with modest-sized houses, presumably for unmarried or single soldiers, while the other side comprised larger houses that accommodated soldiers with families of varying sizes. Despite the size differences, these abodes were fairly distributed among the soldiers and were of similar quality, featuring close to identical layouts. Bedrooms, latrines (medieval versions of toilets or attached outhouses), and food storage, were usually found on the upper floors, whereas the downstairs usually acted as a living room.

The upper deck of the Alcazaba community was designed to cater to the needs of hundreds of soldiers and all their families at once, so it would be furnished accordingly. One could access silos, which were tall towers or pits used for grain storage. Armories were aplenty, built to store stockpiles of weapons, ammunition, tools, and other equipment. A communal oven sat in the middle of Alcazaba, where inhabitants could bake bread and other pastries.

At first glance, Alcazaba might have seemed like any other part of the complex, if not for the perfectly round cavity in the middle of the square, its lid a set of unbudging steel grills lodged firmly into the ground. Only upon closer look would one realize that this was no well or ordinary pit but actually the Alcazaba dungeon. Prisoners were tossed into this well, which ran at least 6 feet deep and only 3 feet wide. This meant there was close to nonexistent wiggle room; criminals were left to roast under the scorching sun, or to shiver their chattering teeth off while drenched in the pouring rain. Later, a portion of the bottom part of the well was removed, which was supposedly either to make room for more prisoners, or to finally allow them some form of shelter from the sun, rain, and other harsh elements. Another interesting hallmark of the Alcazaba was the Torre Blanca, or "Roman tomb," which gifted visitors a divine view of the rest of the complex through the horseshoe-shaped windows.

The 14th century Moorish rulers Muhammed III, Yusuf I, and Muhammed V are most often credited with overseeing the construction of the majority of the structures that can still be seen in the curious complex today. Towards the beginning of the 1300s, Muhammed III ordered a set of blueprints made for the infrastructure of the Medina. He would then employ a separate set of contractors to start work on a collection of mosques and public baths, as well as the Puerta del Vino, or "Wine Gate," and the *rauda*, a sumptuous burial chamber reserved for the sultans.

In 1333, Yusuf I was the first to convert Alhambra into an impressive place for royal residents. That year, the city of Granada would become the official capital of the Nasrid empire. While Ismail I, the sultan before him, along with a few others, had already resided in the renovated rooms of existing towers within Alhambra, it would be Yusuf who spearheaded the construction of the Comares Palace. In time, 2 more well-known palaces that the residents of Granada have come to know and treasure, were also built – the Palace of the Lions and the Partal Palace.

The El Mexuar, commissioned by Ismail, was an "audience chamber," a royal office dedicated to conducting formal interviews and handling business affairs. A few decades later, in the 1330s, the El Mexuar was reassigned as a public reception hall. This particular room hosted one of the most remarkable interiors thanks to the designers' use of vividly colored tile dadoes – wall panels designed differently from those on the ceiling – in geometric patterns. The dainty but ornately detailed carvings on the stucco panels and high ceilings also made it the ideal place for public gatherings and meetings, worthy of the most distinguished members of Granada.

Standing right behind the El Mexuar was Yusuf's brainchild, the Comares Palace, which came complete with a luxurious courtyard and fountain. The exterior of the palace was enhanced with stucco and embellished with intricate etchings. This facade was once painted with a rainbow of colors, but over time, much of the paint has peeled off, and only hints of the once spirited color palette lingers.

This palace was built upon an elevated platform, with 3 steps attached to the front gate, as this was believed to have served as a royal pedestal where the sultan announced decrees and addressed his subjects. By the rear of the palace lives a twisting path, leading to a deluxe roofed patio known as the "Court of the Myrtles." The court contained a stately private pool, and was considered one of the most appealing features in the entire complex.

The Court of the Myrtles

When Yusuf took over, he also demanded the construction of a special room in Comares Tower, which at 45 meters was the tallest in all of Alhambra. There, the Salón de Comares, or "Hall of Ambassadors," was built. Since Yusuf chose this space as his private bedchamber, the designers were confronted with their greatest task yet, but they took the challenge in stride. By the end of the tremendous feat, the salon housed the most spectacular and elaborately detailed of all the architectural and aesthetic designs in the multilevel complex.

Multicolored tiles arranged in a variety of geometric and symmetric patterns were painstakingly adorned on the walls of the spacious and lavishly decorated bedchamber. Colored tiles from this time period would have been produced with the following substances. Ground cobalt was used to create blue tones, and manganese for shades of purple and black. A mixture of copper generated red or green paints, tin for whites, and lead or antimony for yellow tones.

Stucco carvings featuring designs with "curvilinear" patterns, as well as Kufic calligraphy, covered the ceilings. The smooth walls were paved with gold tiles that gleamed under the golden glow of the sunlight trickling in through the lattice grills of the windows mounted high up on the walls. Sets of tall, arched windows fixed with glass that came in floral, geometric, and other Moorish designs allowed even more crisp air and natural light to waft into the room.

The grandness of the Comares Palace also made it the optimal setting for various Moorish ceremonies. Beneath the fine vaulted ceiling, the sultan sat upon a throne in the middle of the room. His throne was highly stylish, but portable, with a low backrest and a comfortable cushion. Its armrests and feet were fashioned from the finest wood, and topped off with more intricate floral carvings.

Standing next to the Comares Palace was the Palace of the Lions. This already astounding structure was further improved upon by Muhammed V in the 14th century. The sultan included a fantastic fountain, which was equipped with an groundbreaking hydraulic system. The fountain was as advanced for its time as it was mesmerizing.

Infrogmation of New Orleans' pictures of the Patio of the Lions

People often slowed their pace as they walked past, awestruck by the giant marble basin sitting upon the backs of a dozen fierce lion statues, which was situated in the intersection that connected a pair of water channels. The stream of the fountain was split into 4 channels that ran in different directions and were met by 4 artificial waterways that transferred the water into small pools. These waterways, or canals, were said to have symbolized the Islamic "River of Heaven."

The Palace of the Lions also boasted a comparable courtyard of its own, as well as its own set of distinctive columns and pavilions. Contractors also made use of *muqarnas,* or "honeycomb vaulting," which were special brackets that formed an 8-pointed star and designed to bolster the vaulted ceilings. Another architectural pattern certain to snag one's attention were the carved rhombuses on the dazzlingly colored walls of the Patio of the Lions, which was linked to the Sala de los Reyes, or the "Hall of the Kings."

On top of the *muqarnas,* the hall was home to numerous alcoves (narrow passageways built into the walls), which provided passersby with an unobstructed view of the courtyard. The hall also featured notable paintings on a trio of domes, which were shaped like ellipses. Rather than paint the images directly onto the ceiling, the art was first sketched onto tanned sheepskin, a widely-used technique for miniature painting, and was later completed with beautiful detail and bright splashes of color.

The artwork had most likely been created during the reigns of Muhammed VII and Yusuf III in the late 14th and early 15th centuries. They depicted the sultans' courtly lives and paid tribute to the first 10 kings of the Nasrid Dynasty, excluding those who had snatched the crown by force. Other scenes were visual portrayals of sultans waving from the tops of their castles, as well as other chivalric and romantic images that told the tales of these beloved kings.

Javier Carro's picture of art on the arches in the Palace of the Lions

The Partal Palace, or Portico Palace, is most renowned for its one-of-a-kind portico, a term that refers to a porch or colonnade leading to the entrance of a building or structure. The portico had 5 arches and provided a splendid view of the sparkling pool sitting in the garden's bosom. Like most other structures in Alhambra, the walls in this palace were coated with plaster. They were then fitted with tiles and friezes, which were horizontal strips on the wall that featured paintings, carvings, or sculptures. The friezes in Portico Palace were bordered with wood, which has led experts to believe that these had been designed during the reign of Muhammad III, sometime in the early 14th century.

The courtyard of the Partal Palace

The sultans' construction projects reached beyond the walls of Alhambra. One such example was the Generalife, which was believed to have been built towards the dawn of the Nasrid reign. This home away from home was a palace for retreats, and was where the sultans often summered. The "*Jannat*" in "*Jannat al-arifa*," which was Generalife in Arabic, meant "paradise" or "garden," aptly describing the wonders behind its walls. It was said that the gardens, water sources, and natural life overflowing in Generalife was simply like no other.

Peter Lorber's picture of the gardens of Genaralife

People were specially hired to tend to the manicuring and cultivating of the flowers, plants, vegetables, and fruits that grew from every corner of Generalife. Exotic critters also took up residence inside the palace. Twittering flocks of nightingales wearing coats of richly-colored feathers also seemed to take a liking to the palace, and became a mascot of sorts. Among the most bewitching gardens in Generalife is one that comes with a narrow patio, as well as a glittering water channel running alongside of it. 2 rows of water fountains emitting its own calming medley can also be found in the same garden.

The Medina, which spanned from the western to the eastern stretch of the complex, was another fully-functioning community of its own. Though the structures here were nowhere near as luxurious as the sultans' quarters, they still suited the standards for the sultan's right hand men.

The Calle Real, which was stowed away in the heart of the Medina, was where mosques, libraries, shops, public baths, and other places of entertainment were found. Engravings found on nearby walls have also alluded to a *madrasa*, or an Islamic college, which is believed to have once lived in the Medina, roughly around the 14th century.

The commercial centers were located in the upper neck of Medina. There, one could find public kilns, another word for ovens used for pottery and baking; a tannery; and even a mint, where inhabitants could produce and stamp their own coins. Compact streets and constricted alleyways connected the supply of houses for servants and court officials. They also bound together the public squares, cisterns, and other structures of the Medina cityscape. Due to the centrality of Medina's location, it guarded Alhambra's most crucial resource – water. The closest source of water was 4 miles away, so a pipeline, later called the *"Acequia del Sultan,"* had to be established to bring the water from outside Alhambra walls into the complex. Water traveled down the pipeline and through a tunnel that had been drilled into Alhambra's defensive walls. The stream's path was then forked into pipelines that rerouted the water to different areas in the complex. The hydraulic system helped to ensure the stability of the water level in the pools at all times.

3 distinguishing architectural features found inside the Alhambra showcased the styles unique to these Moorish designers. The styles were so unique that a term was coined for one of these styles: "Arabesque." The Arabesque motif was characterized by the use of symmetrical and geometrical patterns, often utilized repetitively in their art. D. Jones, author of *Architecture of the Islamic World*, fittingly dissected the Arabesque style with the following statement: "This limitless, rhythmical alteration of movement, conveyed by the reciprocal repetition of curved lines, produces a design that is balanced...and geometric."

Moorish artists were said to have consciously chosen these patterns for a reason, as not unlike Christianity, anything regarded as too "realistic" could be considered idolatrous. Back then, Moorish artists rarely featured human characters in their artwork, as doing so could mean placing oneself in competition with Allah, the untouchable creator of the universe. While most of Alhambra was seasoned with Arabesque touches, the Romans, Byzantines, and Greeks served as the muses for the border designs of vines, and stylized vegetable and fruit patterns.

Another angle that set these Moorish art techniques apart were the calligraphic carvings engraved into the walls in Arabic cursive, most in the form of poems and verses from the Qu'ran. Over 10,000 sets of calligraphic carvings can be found across Alhambra, etched into walls, ceilings, windows, and doorways. Other than verses from the Quran, these inscriptions shared lyrical descriptions of the most prominent features in the room; anecdotes and limericks that told the stories of past sultans and leaders; and other philosophical sayings.

A picture of decorations on an arch

Perhaps the most famous of all the Alhambran inscriptions was the Nasrid motto, which read, "There is no victor but Allah." This phrase was carved hundreds of times onto walls, columns, arches, and tapestries around the complex. Other repeated carvings were single-worded blessings found in the palaces, which included "blessing" and "happiness." These sacred incantations were meant to protect those who resided in the royal quarters – namely, the sultan and his family. Aphorisms were either philosophical or infused with religious tones, such as "Be sparse in words and you will go in peace," "Eternity is an attribute of God," and "Rejoice in good fortune, because Allah helps you."

An example of one of the poignant poems found on Comares Gate reads:

"I am a crown on the front of my door: in me is the West envious of the East.

Al-Gani billah orders me to quickly give way to victory, as soon as it calls.

I am always waiting to see the visage of the king, dawn appearing from the horizon.

May God make his works as beautiful as are his mettle and his figure."

Another describes the features of the room, and simultaneously praises the leadership of Muhammed V, found in the Hall of the Two Sisters:

"I am the garden appearing every morning with adorned beauty;

Contemplate my beauty and you will be penetrated with understanding.

I excel through the generosity of my lord...Muhammed for all who come and go...

In here is a cupola by which its height becomes lost from sight,

Beauty in it appears both concealed and visible..."

A picture of the Hall of the Two Sisters

Gothic and Mudejar Phases

"Burn old wood, read old books, drink old wines, have old friends." – attributed to Alfonso X of Castile

Alfonso X the Wise may have shared his father's passion towards the growth of Seville, as well as his partiality for Moorish art and culture, but the palace left behind by the Muslim rulers failed to meet the king's standards of living and the requirements of the Castilian court. Whereas the Moors preferred more compact spaces with complex, labyrinthine layouts, so as to ensure the peace and solitude needed in meditation, the new occupants of the Alcázar favored proper palatial rooms in both size and grandeur. More importantly, whereas the Moors preferred a relatively uniform look throughout the entirety of their establishments, the Christian monarchs were accustomed to designing and ornamenting the different parts of the palace based on their respective "hierarchical" merits. The governmental wings, for example, would not have warranted as much attention in terms of majesty and detail when compared to the private residences of the royals.

Operating on this logic, Alfonso chose not only to expand the palace but also consciously infused into his new home Gothic elements, or as defined by the *Visual Arts Encyclopedia,* "[architectural features] which linked medieval Romanesque art with the Early Renaissance." Alfonso, like many royals of his time, was especially taken with the fresh aesthetic that aimed to blend the old with the new, a style popularized and imported from France. Furthermore, Gothic art forms were closely affiliated with the Crusaders, meaning his decision to decorate in this style was a sort of homage to Christianity's triumph over Islam. From that point forward, the once Moorish Palace was to be known as the *Palacio Gótico,* or the Gothic Palace.

Authenticity being one of Alfonso's priorities, Castilian, French, and other European architects and artists with shimmering resumes, including the very masons who assembled the immaculate interior and naves of the breathtaking Burgos Cathedral, were employed for the task. Renovations began on the 22nd of March, 1254, and the laborers' first assignment was to build a channel that would transport water from the Caños de Carmona into the Alcázar. Future sovereigns, such as Emperor Carlos V (Charles V) and King Felipe II, renovated and added their own touches to the Gothic Palace in the 16th century, but most of the original ground floor was kept as it was.

Holy Roman Emperor Charles V

The ceramic tile plinths, or "dados," that adorned the baseboards bordering the bottom halves of the palace walls, like those found in the radiant Halls of Carlos V, were designed by Cristóbal de Augusta, a potter from Navarre who was married to the daughter of a manufacturer of malioca ("tin-glazed earthenware") tiles. These plinths, often likened to tapestries, comprised two upper friezes, a lower frieze, and a central panel boxed in by its own borders, and separated by grotesques (an artistic style that combines human and animal forms with foliage). The lower strip features pairs of animals, such as lions, tigers, dragons, and mythical beasts, facing away from each other. Curly-haired cherubs, colorful birds, and serpents garnish the bottom half of the upper frieze, while the top half, on the other hand, is embellished with angels and fair maidens clutching onto the crest of the Spanish Crown, as well as columns displaying a banner with the words "Plus Ultra" ("Further Beyond)," the personal motto of Carlos V.

This sensational tile artwork is only one of the hallmarks of Carlos V's stunning hall. The place is brought to life with its Gothic vaulted ceilings and their striking wooden trimmings, and the floor-length springline windows, which bathe the walls and floors with brilliant natural light and allow those on the inside to admire the view of the gardens. Back in the day, those on the side of the palace overlooking the *Patio del Crucero* often wandered out to the upper-story walkway in the middle of the afternoon, chatting away as they snacked on sweet oranges freshly plucked from the trees within reach.

The Sala de las Bóvedas in the Gothic Palace

The Gothic Palace is also famed for the Chapel of San Clemente, installed by Alfonso in 1271. Little of the original place of worship, however, remains. The chapel is now dominated by an ornate wooden altarpiece, designed by 18th century artist Diego de Castillejo, depicting the cloaked Virgin of Antigua carrying Jesus as a child, and a white rose. Three winged angels hover over the Virgin, brandishing a bejeweled crown in their hands. Above the altarpiece itself, is a round stained glass window with the royal insignia of the Spanish Crown, wreathed by blue, violet, and yellow flowers. A rusty organ, mirror, "confessional armchair," and a medieval iron chandelier used in the chapel centuries ago can now be found on display in the Alcázar.

The only other major addition made before the reign of Pedro the Cruel in the mid-14ᵗʰ century was the *Sala de Justica*. Construction of this "Justice Chamber" was commissioned by King Alfonso XI, the great-grandson of Alfonso X, supposedly to commemorate his victory against the Muslims during the Battle of Salado. Builders expanded upon and revamped the *mexuar*, or public reception hall of the former Moorish palace, which was situated next to the *Patio del Yeso*. The original room had been built with the Persian *qubba*, or domed mausoleums typically used in Islamic worship; though the squareness of the space and the baroque latticework with the 8-pointed star on the ceiling were preserved, the floor tiles were replaced with warmer, reddish-brown colors. A small, circular pool rimmed with gray marble, which was hooked up to the pond in the *Patio del Yeso*, was also installed.

It was here that the Moorish Imperial Council, otherwise known as the "Council of Viziers," convened during Saracen times. When Pedro was handed the royal scepter in 1350, the *Sala de Justica* became a courtroom of sorts, where he pardoned and meted out punishments to those who he branded guilty.

Despite Pedro's alleged barbarism and the countless horror stories that continue to sully his name to this day, he was responsible for some of the most regal rooms and qualities of the Alcázar. Rarely mentioned are Pedro's surprisingly progressive foreign policies; apart from his deep admiration of Moorish and Berber culture, his cabinet was staffed with as many Moriscos as Christians, as well as plenty of Muslims and even a smattering of Jews. His unlikely alliance with the Moors bore so much weight, in fact, that he even secured a covenant of mutual assistance with more than one Nasrid Sultan from Granada so as to get a leg up on his local enemies.

Pedro's rapport with the Muslims was ultimately what allowed him to construct what many claim to be the most spectacular part of the fortress: the *Palacio del Rey Don Pedro,* or the "Palace of King Peter I." The palace, the only structure crafted from scratch – foundations included – is often referred to as the "Mudejar Palace." The term "*mudejar,*" stems from the Arabic word, "*mudajian,*" or "domesticated," and denotes the "use of Islamic motifs in non-Muslim settings." In this case, the "*mudejar*" art style marries both Islamic and Christian elements, producing one beautiful fusion of a product. *Sevillano* columns (dappled marble columns crowned with gilded moldings), poly-lobed arches, thin green tiles separating blocks of voussoirs, and ornamental stucco in "sebka patterns (a network of diamond shapes)," as well as tiles, friezes, and panels with human and animal representation in Moorish art styles, are just some of the Mudejar features of the palace.

One of the gates in the Palace of Peter of Castile

Pedro's decision to depart from the Gothic art style may have also been politically motivated. While Pedro was about as Catholic as other Castilian kings, he supposedly harbored a deep resentment for the French Church, taking great offense to the Avignon popes' illegitimate children, advocacy for simony, indulgences, and other corrupt practices. He thought the Gothic art form bland, banal, and more alien than it was exotic.

Like Alfonso X, Pedro aimed for authenticity. Rather than employing random artists and laborers and instructing them to emulate Moorish aesthetics, Pedro reached out to Emir Muhammad V, one of his closest political allies, and requested from him an assemblage of the most stellar Moorish craftsmen. Most of the exceptionally talented artists, artisans, and architects who came over from Granada, Toledo, and the outskirts of Seville had personally worked on the last round of construction of the splendid Alhambra.

The Arabic and Latin inscriptions carved onto the walls and the entrance of the palace, highlighted by bright cobalt-blue tiles, are perhaps one of the best examples of cultural synthesis. "The empire of God," reads the Arabic phrase repetitiously engraved between the columns on the middle level of the palace facade. Above the three sets of poly-lobed arched windows is a blue-and-white panel with the words, "There is no conqueror but God," stamped onto it in Kufic script. Finally, the following Latin passage is etched onto the decorative strip around this panel: "The highest, noblest, and most powerful conqueror, Don Pedro, by God's grace King of Castile and Leon [sic], has caused these Alcázares and palaces and these facades to be built, which was done in the year 1364." Other epigraphs one might find in Pedro's palace include "Glory to our Lord, the Sultan Peter!," "May Allah Protect Him!," and "Only Allah is Victorious."

A picture of Arabic inscriptions glorifying the Christian rulers

Those who pieced together the *Palacio del Rey Don Pedro* plotted the structure in two parts. Half of the establishment, which houses the *Patio de las Doncellas*, or the "Damsels' Courtyard," was to be open to the public. The other half, built around the *Patio de las Muñecas,* or the "Dolls' Courtyard," was to be exclusive to the royals and other private parties.

The Patio de las Doncellas courtyard

If someone wished to access the palace, one had to pass through the *Patio de la Montería,* the "Hunting Courtyard." As hinted by its name, the courtyard was where Pedro and other royals gathered with their hunting circles before their expeditions. This was also the central *patio* of the Alcázar, and functions as the primary junction between the fortress' palaces. The courtyard was also home to a fabulous collection of remarkable flora. The walls crawled with curtains of ivy and moss. Towering cypress, palm, and fruitful banana trees sprouted from the fertile earth. Sprinkled in between them were myrtle hedges, pomegranate shrubs, floppy elephant ears that provided plenty of shade, sweeping squares of yellow, fuchsia, red, and orange lantanas, and thorny blankets of pink, red, and violet rose bougainvilleas, to name a few.

A passageway from the Hunting Courtyard, paved with colorful chessboard tiles, leads to the *Patio de las Doncellas*, also known as the "Maidens' Courtyard." This *patio,* which serves as the main courtyard of Gothic Palace, was rehabilitated, redecorated, and rechristened by Pedro sometime in the 1370s. Its name was directly inspired by a myth from antiquity in which the Christian kings of Iberia were made to pay an annual tribute of 100 virgins (half of them of noble birth) to the Islamic Emirate of Cordoba in exchange for a guarantee of their continued independence. Daniel Eisenberg, one of the authors of the *Encyclopedia of Medieval Iberia*, has denounced this as no more than an urban legend, propaganda perpetuated by Christian rulers and the 13th century Church that aimed to galvanize the Christians' ultimately successful efforts to reclaim southern Spain.

The four pools in the Maidens' Courtyard, which represent the four rivers of heaven in the Quran, as well as the four continents known to mankind during Moorish times, were among one of the major features Pedro chose to preserve. Visitors say one can best appreciate the courtyard by sitting upon a tiled recess, or alcove, in the corner of the garden. Only then can one truly marvel at the captivating arcades, the "star-patterned Mudejar *azulejos* (blue-and-white ceramic tile work often found in Spain and Portugal), " the spellbinding patterns carved into the moldings of the arches, and the fragrant cluster of orange trees in one sitting.

The courtyard provided a grand backdrop for numerous meetings, feasts, and friendly gatherings between the Christian royals and their officials; conferences were also held in the Ambassadors' Hall, the Room of the Ceiling of Felipe II, and the Room of the Half Crane, which surrounded the patio. Towards the end of the 1500s, three of the pools, as well as a few sections of the gardens were covered with marble plates and padded down with fertile soil, creating a long and narrow reflecting pool in the center of the courtyard. The gallery of white "semicircular arches," complete with matching slender columns and railing on the second floor of the open-air *patio*, was constructed during the time of King Charles I.

The Castilian kings' private courtyard, the *Patio de las Muñecas,* is visibly marked by a more personal touch. Some say it was designed specifically to suit the exquisite tastes of Pedro's queen, though it's not clear exactly which queen this was. The pretty rectangular *patio* is flanked on 4 sides by a cream-colored series of "ruffled," or poly-lobed arches and diamond-latticed haunches, shored up by short columns of white, pink, and black marble from the city of Madinat Al-Zahra.

The *patio* was given another major makeover between the years of 1847 and 1855, a project directed by esteemed woodcarver José Gutiérrez de la Vega. The floral-eqsque indentations and "cellular" carvings (*muqarnas*) on the cornices, or the molding above the arches and haunches, were added during this time. The "Neo-Mudejar" mezzanine, located between the first floor and the grilled windows on the second story, was built shortly thereafter. When the aged columns of the courtyard eventually began to show signs of cracks and crumbling, the marble specialist José Barradas was hired to replace them.

A self portrait of José Gutiérrez de la Vega

17th century historian Rodrigo Caro was among the first to ponder the etymology of the courtyard's name. The Courtyard of the Dolls, insisted Caro, was dubbed as such either because of its dainty size and character or the royal children's tendency to play with their dolls in the courtyard. Nowadays, it is believed that the courtyard was named after the minuscule chubby doll faces subtly sculpted into the curves of the courtyard's arches and pillars.

The nine smiling doll faces peppered throughout the *patio* are only a few of the Easter eggs concealed within the Alcázar. One should also be on the lookout for the golden peacocks camouflaged in the foliage swirls above the triple arch in the Ceiling Room of Philip II. Those able to discover all the Easter eggs unaided, say local mystics, are either blessed with child or good fortune.

Later Castilian kings also renamed the *Puerta de la Montería* the *"Puerta del Leon."* The *puerta,* or the "Lion's Gate" – which leads to the *Patio del Leon,* a protruding segment wedged between the *Sala de la Justica* and the *Cuarto del Almirante* (Admiral's Room) – is essentially the main entrance to the entire fortress. A black arch door was installed in the center of the crimson gate. Above the door is a tile panel – a José Gestoso original – showcasing a crowned heraldic lion with a lolling tongue, wielding a golden cross with one claw, and stomping upon what appears to be the pole of a blue flag with the other. A white sash draped around the lion, bearing the Gothic script, *"Ad Utrumque,"* or "Prepared for All," completes the picture. The

Triana tiles used in this piece were sourced from the Sevillean ceramics factory of José Mensaque y Vera.

Ian Tom Ferry's picture of the Lion's Gate

The *Los Baños de Doña María de Padilla,* a network of baths-turned-rainwater tanks underneath the *Patio del Crucero,* is yet another notable sector of the Alcázar that Pedro the Cruel had refurbished.

Even in the early years of his reign, it appeared as if Pedro had learned nothing from the marital indiscretions of his father, though in his defense, the situation was considerably more complicated. In 1353, Pedro halfheartedly exchanged his wedding vows with Blanche of Bourbon in Valladolid. This was a calculated arrangement orchestrated by Pedro's mother, Maria of Portugal, to ensure a sound relationship with the French Crown. Not only was Blanche's pedigree favorable – she was the first cousin of King John II, and the daughter of Duke Pedro I of Bourbon, the great-grandson of King Louis IX, and Isabel de Valois, the granddaughter of King Philip III – the fair-haired 14-year-old was sharp-witted, well-educated, and spiritually irrepressible.

However, unbeknownst to the queen, Pedro had already married another noblewoman – a sultry, dark-haired beauty by the name of Maria de Padilla. Though this was a fact Pedro vehemently denied, he deserted Blanche and fled to the arms of his "mistress" less than 72 hours after his marriage. Like father, like son, Pedro had a bunch of children with his paramour, a total of 14 to be exact, but only 4 would reach adulthood.

As one might expect, Pedro's impulsive divorce from Blanche incited uproar among the upper echelons of Spain and France, and on top of that, the temperamental king imprisoned his former bride. Humiliated and outraged by Pedro's actions, his mother and Aunt Leonor attempted to guilt and hector him into taking back Blanche, in no small part due to the fact they were deeply anxious about the prospect of Maria's Castilian and Portuguese relatives "stealing" the prestigious titles and privileges that belonged to them. But Pedro, the iron-willed and brutish sovereign that he was, was not to be trifled with, and anyone who dared to speak ill of the love of his life was marched to the gallows or executed in some other manner, no questions asked.

In 1361, the most radiant light in Pedro's life was extinguished when 27-year-old Maria passed away, supposedly due to a particularly ferocious outbreak of the plague. Her body was initially buried in the convent she erected, but she was later laid to rest alongside the royals in the Seville Cathedral.

Curiously, there exists another version of Pedro and Maria's love story floating around, one defiled by a dark twist. Maria, claim some chroniclers, was already a wife when Pedro first laid his eyes on her, and it was Pedro himself who arranged the murder of Maria's husband. The inconsolable and heartbroken Maria enrolled at the Santa Clara convent in a remote part of the city in a bid to find solace, but to her dismay, Pedro tracked her down. Her royal stalker was relentless, even going so far as to build a tower next to the convent for the sole purpose of spying on her. When the traumatized Maria was eventually driven to delirium by the merciless harassment, the unhinged young woman stumbled into the underground baths of the Alcázar. Once she had lured Pedro into the baths, she hoisted a barrel of boiling oil over her head and poured out its contents, willingly scalding her own face and chest. It was only then that Pedro showed some semblance of remorse, after which he finally retired his "romantic" pursuit of her and permitted her to open the Convent of Santa Inés. As darkly gripping as this tale is, only part of it is true, because while such tragic events did unfold, it happened to Maria Fernandez Coronel, most likely after the death of Maria de Padilla.

At the end of the day, of all the women in Pedro's life, it was Maria de Padilla who left the most indelible imprint. As such, to honor the memory of his one true love, Pedro renamed the part of the palace Maria frequented most after her.

Sevilla. Alcázar, Salon de D/Maria de Padillas.

An 1895 picture

Indeed, the Alcázar played host to several pivotal moments throughout the controversial life of Pedro the Cruel. The *Sala de Justica*, for one, was the setting for a string of unfortunate events, each disturbing in its own right. Three years before the death of Pedro's precious Maria, the vindictive king ordered the death of his half-brother, Fadrique Alfonso, in that very room. Defenders of Pedro's actions assert that the sentencing, while brutal, was necessary; not only was Pedro eliminating a political rival, he was saving his own skin, for Fadrique and his retinue were in the process of plotting his murder. Others claim that the murder was strictly personal, and that Fadrique fathered an illegitimate child with his former sister-in-law, Blanche. Pedro may have had zero romantic interest in her, but he would not stand for such blatant disrespect.

Whatever the case, on the 29th of May, 1358, Fadrique walked into the Alcázar for what he thought would be a nice dinner with his brother, but en route to the dining hall, Fadrique was suddenly waylaid by one of the guards and shepherded towards the *sala*. Fadrique staggered out of the Justice Hall and attempted to make a break for it, but Pedro, as the story goes, soon caught up to him and dragged him back to the *sala*. Flushed and out of breath, a stuttering Fadrique pleaded for his life and strove once again to bolt out of the room, but before his foot could make it past the threshold, Pedro crept up behind him and shattered his skull with a mace. That same evening, Pedro and his guards circled the palace, hunting down what was left of Fadrique's retinue.

When Pedro returned to the *sala* and found Fadrique curled up on the floor, motionless but still breathing, he nonchalantly handed a dagger to a nearby page and had him finish the job. One witness wrote, "After this was done, the King sat down to eat where the master lay dead..." The dark, reddish spot now seen on the marble floor of the *sala* is said to be the remnants of Fadrique's blood.

The Fall of Granada

"Such is the happiness of the world, and therefore the ignorant are allured by it, as fish are drawn to their destruction by a glittering bait." – Venerable Louis of Granada

Meanwhile, the Reconquista movement had failed to simmer down; on the contrary, it did just the opposite. The Christians continued their attempts to reclaim Al-Andalus from the Muslims, realizing the fears of a now long-gone Muhammed I. Close to 8 decades after Muhammed and his forces paraded into Granada, the Christians contemplated the capture of the city for the first time. By then, the Christians had already secured Sevilla, Jaen, and Cordoba, among other towns. Some of these recaptured lands were also allotted to 2 other kings: Jaime I of Aragon, and Alfonso III of Portugal. By the time the 14th century rolled around, the only territory that remained in the hands of Muslim authority was Granada, and in it, the coveted Alhambra palace and fortress.

At this point in time, the crown of Castile was plagued by internal conflict. Trouble began to brew as King Alfonso X drew closer to his final breath. His second son, Sancho IV, had cut in front of the rightful heirs in the line to the throne. This was the first strike, earning not only the wrath of his dying father as he lay in his deathbed but the people's resentment. In 1295, upon Sancho's untimely death, his 9-year-old son, Fernando IV, was thrust onto the throne. Rival leaders from Aragon and Portugal leaped at the opportunity to take the throne from the child. Infante don Juan, the brother of Sancho, vied for the throne, hoping to thwart Fernando's coronation by condemning his deceased brother's marriage to Queen Maria de Molina.

In time, Queen Maria managed to retain her son's place on the throne, but in September of 1312, Fernando himself would meet a premature death before his 27th birthday, leaving his 11-month-old son, Alfonxo XI, in his place. This provoked yet another power struggle, a pattern that would be followed for the next 3 years. The 3 contestants who were now contending for the throne were Queen Maria, the grandmother of the toddler king hopeful; Infante don Pedro, the great-uncle; and Infante don Juan, the paternal uncle. In 1315, the trio finally settled their differences and agreed to rule as a team, with territories equally divvied up between them.

Interestingly enough, while the Christians' drive remained as sharp as ever, the crown-snatching shenanigans had left Castile weak and disoriented. A year later, Pedro and his army infiltrated Granada. The Nasrid forces, who had failed to predict the seemingly spontaneous attack, were quickly defeated, and were left with no alternative but to surrender one of the castles in Alhambra. Historians now believe that the Castilians would have easily been able to progress much further, were it not for Juan, who had attempted to declare himself the sole monarch of Castile with Pedro out of the way. The moment Pedro learned of this, he retreated to Castile to call an immediate stop to those proceedings.

3 years later, Pedro and Juan ceased their squabbling. It was seemingly only then they realized that if they wanted Granada, a solid partnership had to be created. Thus, on June 25, 1319, Juan and Pedro's forces barged into Granada once more, this time electing to enter via the Sierra de Elvira Hill. To their astonishment, a Nasrid army was already laying in wait for them, armed and ready. The opposing forces charged at one another, and it would not take long before the pendulum swung in the Moors' direction. The Castilian forces were visibly out of their comfort zone. They were not used to combat in the blistering heat, and soon became dehydrated and distracted. In the heat of the pandemonium, the Castilian forces were split down the middle, making it easier for the Nasrid forces to isolate and subdue the invaders. Pedro himself was ejected from his horse, promptly snapping his neck as he crashed to the ground.

Pedro's body was later supposedly recovered by the Nasrids, and the corpse of the lifeless monarch was supposedly skinned, stuffed, and put on display. Juan, heavily wounded, managed to stagger out of the gates, but soon, he either bled out from his wounds or succumbed to infection. Other accounts stated that Juan was not wounded but instead died of a broken heart.

Following the fall of the Christian kings in battle, the Castilian forces eventually followed suit. All in all, up to 50,000 men were said to have died in battle. Again, these figures, which were plucked from the accounts of medieval chroniclers, must be sprinkled with several grains of salt.

Bombardments from Christian invaders aside, life within Alhambra was rife with its own share of internal struggles. One of the most pressing problems was the numerous assassination plots birthed behind these walls, both effective and ineffective. It seemed as if the Moorish sultans could do nothing to escape this unbreakable streak of misfortune. Between the first 9 sultans, from Muhammed I to Ismail II, only one, who was incidentally – or maybe, coincidentally – deposed, died a natural "white death," passing away in his sleep unperturbed. 7 were assassinated, and one was killed in a horrific accident.

In 1333, 15-year-old Yusuf I had succeeded his brother, Muhammed IV, at the throne. To begin with, the young sultan was regarded as dim and childish, equipped with only a "royal writ [that] ran no further than the power to decide what he would have for dinner." Yet what he lacked, he made up for with his affinity with architecture and design. Lamentably, his ambitious projects came to a skidding halt. In 1354, as the sultan prayed in the Mosque of Granada, he was stabbed to death by a mentally ill slave.

Yusuf had preferred to have his son Ismail II as his successor, but the senior statesmen chose to fill the royal seat with Muhammed V instead. Muhammed shared a father with Ismail, but was born by a slave. Though the people were still quivering from the news of the assassination, Muhammed V proved to be one of the finest rulers of the European emirates. Of course, his rule, though popular with most, was not well-received by all. Just 5 years into his reign, a new set of plotters concocted a plan for his demise in the hopes of seizing Alhambra for themselves. One fateful Ramadan, a band of conspirators, armed with knives and a deadly determination, stealthily crept up to Muhammed in the mosque. The sultan, who had heard the approaching footsteps in the nick of time, managed to escape.

These conspirators had been hired by his half-brother, Ismail, most known for being overweight and effeminate. In Muhammed V's absence, Ismail slithered into the throne. Ismail's reign would also be abruptly cut short when he was murdered by his cousin, a hashish connoisseur with possible Tourette's syndrome. This cousin soon declared himself the great sultan, Muhammed VI.

The cycle seemed interminable. In 1360, with the support of Peter the Cruel, King of Castile, Muhammed V returned. It was then that Peter himself personally killed Muhammed VI with a lance, vacating the throne once more for Muhammed V. These unabating tensions led one 15th century Muslim scholar to remark, "Is Granada not enclosed between a violent sea enemy and an enemy terrible in arms, both of which press on its people day and night?"

As Moorish Spain headed into the 15th century, juggling these mounting internal and external dilemmas, the sultans had no choice but to divert their attention to the increasing number of Christian raiders looking to yank the rug from underneath them. Thus, construction and renovations on the Alhambra were put on a hiatus. With all progress on ongoing construction projects on the complex either stalled or canceled, it was time to face the towering tide of the Reconquista head on.

Since they had almost effortlessly defeated the Christian invaders in 1319, the Moors thought this would be little more than a cakewalk. They were sorely mistaken. In 1477, Sultan Abu I-Hasan Ali incurred the rage of their Castilian allies when he refused to acknowledge the Crown of Castile, or pay the taxes required of him. To further flaunt his defiance, in 1481, without warning, Ali unleashed an army in the Castilian city of Zahara de la Sierra. There, Ali's men exterminated hundreds of innocent Christians, young and old, and reclaimed the city as Moorish territory. Many believe this event was what spurred the Islamophobia of Queen Isabella I of Castile. The queen began to plot her retribution, vowing that one day, she would take back Granada and unify all of Castile under Catholicism.

Isabella

As the Castilian monarch devised her plan, Sultan Ali's son by his blood relative, Aixa, took matters into his own hands. With the aid of the Castilians, Muhammed XII, otherwise known as "King Boabdil," booted his father from the throne in 1487. He then did some damage control, once again allowing Granada to be reverted to a tributary state under Castilian authority. Boabdil was also instructed to keep his hands clean from the Siege of Málaga that same year, which saw the city reclaimed by the Christian monarchs.

By 1491, Granada was back to being the one and only city under Moorish authority, and the Alhambra remained unscathed and intact. As a result, Boabdil was left with the impression that he had quelled the anger of the Castilian monarchs. Little did he know, he would be the last Moorish sultan in Alhambra.

The Castilian revenge plot was buttressed by one secret ingredient – the union of Isabella I and Ferdinand of Aragon. This in effect merged the 2 strongest and most influential Christian kingdoms in the Iberian Peninsula, rendering them unstoppable. Unbeknownst to Boabdil, the monarchs' support had come with a veiled motive, stirring up more conflict within the Moors and enfeebling the foundations for the kingdom. They had hoped that the sultan would waltz right into the next phase of their plan, and that, he did. Boabdil now held no control over any other territories outside of Granada.

Ferdinand

In 1482, Pope Sixtus IV had issued a papal bull calling for a crusade against the Muslims of Granada, and in 1491, less than a decade later, Boabdil received a letter from the Castilian monarchs. The sultan unfurled the letter, only to have his jaw drop as he read the monarchs' message. He reread the letter and rubbed at his eyes furiously, but the sentiment was crystal clear – the Castilians wanted him to surrender the city he had just obtained. It was at this point that Boabdil would have realized that he had been nothing but an idle instrument in the plan, but there was nothing he could do about it.

While the odds were stacked against him, Boabdil would not give up without a fight. He pleaded for support from leaders in Islamic North African territories, but only one would respond with a pitiful navy fleet from the Ottomans, which did little damage, if any at all. The Castilian armies continued to pour in, and by the end of the year, Ferdinand and Isabella's forces were camped out all throughout and outside of Alhambra. Nowhere left to turn, Boabdil admitted defeat and surrendered in November 1491, grudgingly signing a treaty to these terms.

On January 2, 1492, the treaty officially went into effect. Castilian forces flooded the city of Granada and confiscated Alhambra, securing the last Muslim-owned state in the Al-Andalus. By noon that morning, the Christian soldiers had evicted most of its previous residents. Moorish flags were removed and replaced with Christian and Castilian flags, and banners strung up in the tallest towers. Most symbolic of all was the giant silver cross that was placed on the highest roof of the Comares Tower, sending out an unmistakable message: the Castilians, along with Catholicism, were here to stay.

On the 30th of July that same year, as told in the diary of Christopher Columbus, the Castilians published an edict that expelled close to 200,000 Jewish people from Spain. Tens of thousands of these refugees died en route to their new destinations. This pivotal expulsion was one of the "pet projects" backed by the Spanish Inquisition. In this petrifying climate, the Muslims of Granada dared not leave their homes. Later that day, Boabdil was driven out of Alhambra. It was said that upon his exit, he cocked his head back to steal a final glimpse of the palace and fortress, only to be reprimanded by his scowling mother, who snapped, "Do not cry like a woman for that which you could not defend as a man."

Upon the outset of this unfamiliar reign, the Muslims were relieved to hear that freedom of worship would be tolerated, and certain leniency would be granted to them to ease them into the new rule. Only, the Castilians would soon fall short on their word. Following a foiled rebellion in the late 1490s, Queen Isabella announced that she would be revoking all laws of tolerance against the Muslims. From 1502 onward, Muslims who wished to avoid execution were presented with 2 choices – convert to Christianity, or leave. Hundreds of thousands fled from Granada, mostly to Africa, while others embraced their new Christian faiths as "Moriscos," as the Spanish called them. A small fraction stayed behind, taking their worship underground.

Authorities placed the Moriscos under strict surveillance, and at the same time, were on the constant lookout for secret Muslims. On Thursday nights and Friday mornings, Moriscos were made to leave their doors open, so that passing soldiers could inspect their houses. Any Morisco who was seen bathing or thought to be suspiciously clean would be apprehended, as Muslim tradition required baths before prayer congregations on Fridays. Those caught red-handed with a Quran were slain on the spot. Stories also surfaced about Castilians kidnapping Muslim children to raise them as Christians behind closed doors.

The Muslims suffered increasingly suffocating restrictions. They were buried under hefty taxes and prohibited from wearing Muslim garb. They were to speak in only Spanish, and those that could not were to find a way to grasp the language within a 3 year period. Many saw their properties seized by Castilian authorities. All Muslim documents were declared null and void.

Even so, what was left of the quickly diminishing Muslims managed to stay in the shadows, and they survived under this brutal authority for over a century, until the new Christian authorities put another foot down by ordering all Moriscos out of their land. For 3 days in 1609, all the Moriscos were forced to pack their belongings and board ships destined for the Ottoman Empire or other North African destinations.

By 1614, almost all the Moriscos had vanished, and the flickering flames of Islam on the Iberian Peninsula were extinguished.

Once Alhambra was under Christian management, a makeover was in order. In the weeks following the conquest of Granada, many of the structures in Granada had their coats of bright Arabesque paints and designs scrubbed and filed off. The freshly sanded facades were then awoken with whitewash, a cost-effective mixture of lime and water used to paint walls a pristine white. The Moorish-style furniture was dismantled and replaced with house fittings and fixtures that better suited the conflicting tastes of the new rulers.

The Christians launched a campaign to remove all traces of the Muslim presence to the best of their ability. Mosques and bathhouses were torn down and rebuilt as churches, convents, and monasteries. In place of the grand mosque stood a stately new cathedral. This same cathedral has since been replaced with the Church of Santa Maria de la Alhambra.

Between the years of Charles I's (aka Charles V, the emperor of the Holy Roman empire) reign from 1516 to 1556, a series of construction projects executed on his behalf saw the destruction of a vast portion of Alhambra. The new structures established upon these empty lots would be more in line with the Renaissance style that was especially popular during this period. Charles V would also later call for the demolition of a Moorish winter palace so that he could build another Renaissance-inspired structure in its place, but this project was ultimately abandoned.

Charles V

The most memorable of the emperor's architectural ventures was the Palacio de Carlos V, or in English, the "Palace of Charles V." Upon visiting Alhambra in 1526, the emperor swiftly fell smitten with the complex. It was then decided that a new home would be established to hold all the comforts, needs, and desires of his family, standards that had yet to be fulfilled in any of his multiple homes. Bearing this in mind, his purpose was not to establish his imperial capital in Alhambra, but was to create a vacation home where his family could rest in between stops during his tour around the continent.

The project had been authorized as early as 1527, when Pedro Machuca Toledo, a pupil of Michelangelo and a veteran architect with a specialty in Renaissance and Romanesque styles, was hired to head the project. All the same, this immense undertaking would only come to completion centuries later, due to revolts, lack of financing, and other obstacles that stood in the way. The 2nd Marquis of Mondejar and Governor of Alhambra, Luis Hartado de Mendoza y Pacheco, was tasked with accumulating the funds needed for the project.

Fernando Martin's picture of the southern façade of the palace

Fernando Martin's picture of the palace's courtyard

This was done by magnifying Moorish taxes that allowed them to keep certain cherished customs. When even these taxes proved insufficient for the costly project, they extracted funds from the Moorish castle, the Alcázar of Sevilla, as well as the profits from sugars and other goods produced locally in Granada. When Toledo died in June of 1550, the torch of project manager was passed onto a number of highly qualified and respected artists, including Juan de Orea, who had headed the construction of the Cathedral of Granada.

Today, this striking square palace stretches 63 meters wide and stands 17 meters high, and it is home to a beautiful circular patio with 2 levels. Only the southern and western portions of the palace facade were enhanced with decorations and the rest untouched, as they were linked to other palaces in Alhambra that were out of his jurisdiction. Architectural traits in this palace included touches of bronze, as well as double-fluted columns and Corinthian pillars. As opposed to arches and squares, windows were rounded.

A carving on the facade of the palace wove the tale of the emperor's vision for his reign. A pair of goddesses clothed in flowing robes are seen with an olive branch in one hand as they balance a crowned globe and the pillars of Hercules with their other. To the bottom corners on either side of the carving, 2 winged angels are seen brandishing a torch and setting a pile of weapons ablaze, as if to demonstrate that war was no longer needed because the emperor had brought with him universal peace.

After the expulsion of the Jews and Moors, the Alcazaba fortress was upgraded to accommodate modern military methods. Towers were either renovated and added onto existing ones, or new ones were constructed. For example, the semicircular tower known as the Torre del Cubo, or "Turret Tower," was later built in the base of the Torre del Homenaje as an additional means of defense. Around this time, the Gunpowder Tower was also converted to a stockroom for the hoarding of more artillery and other equipment.

Excluding the aesthetic alterations made to the place, the Castilians made several other changes. With every last one of the Moorish residents gone, the Christian monarchs failed to make any sense of the complicated Nasrid irrigation and water system. Thus, they had to create one of their own.

With most of the Kufic inscriptions erased, new slogans of the Christian kings were carved into and hung up all over Alhambra. Among these phrases was "Plus Ultra," a Latin phrase that meant "further beyond." Holes were also bored into patches of tiles on the ground to create vents, allowing warm air from the underground heating system to travel throughout the rooms of the renovated places.

The Christians, who were every bit as enchanted with the Alhambra as the Moors had been, were determined to stay. In fact, Isabella and Ferdinand had requested to be buried within the grounds of Alhambra. The Capilla Real, the mausoleum for the Castilian crowns, was built in 1504, and its chapel was added in 1517. Today, Isabella's crown, scepter, and paintings, as well as Ferdinand's sword and other royal keepsakes, can be found in a museum on the site. The bodies of the monarchs now rest in the mausoleum, its exterior decorated with crests featuring the letters "F" and "Y" (for Ysabel).

Renaissance and Revivals

"The distance is great from the firm belief to the realization from concrete experience." – attributed to Queen Isabella I of Castile

In 1503, 11 years after Christopher Columbus reached the New World, the city of Seville was granted exclusive trading rights with the foreign land. To oversee, police, and ensure the stability of this valuable new business relationship, Queen Isabella I of Castile established the *Casa de Contratacion*, or in English, the "House of Trade." This commercial nerve center was to be headed by the queen's personal chaplain and the supervisor of Columbus' voyages, Juan Rodriguez de Fonseca.

The original *Casa de Contratacion* was raised by Alfonso X in the Royal Shipyards, but Isabella – who recognized the Sevillean port's susceptibility to floods, which often damaged much of the merchandise – chose to relocate the institution to the south of the Hunting Courtyard in the Real Alcázar. For the next two centuries, the *Casa* regulated the naval traffic, vetting passengers and goods alike as they traveled from and into the port. Even missionaries journeying to the Indies to the spread Christianity were given a healthy once-over.

Since the Castilian crown viewed the American colonies as their rightful possessions, the chief objective of the *Casa* was to funnel as much of the profits as they could into the royal treasury. In order to do so, the institution had to maintain a firm grip around the commercial maritime activities on a daily basis. At first glance, the process seemed simple enough, as Sevillean merchant vessels were to land in their designated ports in the Americas, load the New World cargo into the vessels, and return to Seville. The uphill battle lay in ensuring the smooth completion of these scheduled deliveries. Fastidious officers employed by the *Casa* worked behind the scenes expeditiously, drawing up and reading reports, crunching numbers, and remedying unavoidable mishaps.

Renowned Italian explorer Amerigo Vespucci, the first Westerner to identify North and South America as "distinct continents," was appointed Chief Navigator of the *Casa* in 1508. Vespucci, who was at the time operating a flourishing Florentine business house in Seville, was well-versed in both the sea and business, making him the ideal candidate for the job. He was charged with granting licenses to captains and charting comprehensive maps of trading routes, as well as territories abroad.

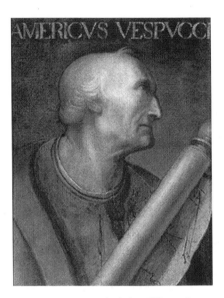

A contemporary depiction of Vespucci

The *Casa* also mustered an armed fleet that chaperoned these merchant vessels to and from their expeditions, staving off pirates and other enemy ships. They also assisted these vessels during storms, salvaging a good chunk of the otherwise doomed commodities on more than one occasion. Working at the *Casa* was a thankless job, but the Sevillean merchants had these employees to thank for making certain that shipments of olives, ceramics, wheat, and leather goods departed from the local port in a timely manner. Likewise, the *Casa's* sailors and employees ensured Seville's safe reception of the gold and silver bullion mined from Mexico and Bolivia, which ignited something of a gold rush in the mid-16th century. To put this into further perspective, the annual value of the gold and silver imports was placed at about 1 million pesos in 1530, but by 1595, that number had skyrocketed to 35 million.

Numerous rooms and halls within the Alcázar were set aside for the use of the *Casa de Contratacion*. Such spaces included the Courtyard of the House of Trade, a private chapel, and the *Salón de Emajadores*. The *Salón*, also known as the "Hall of Ambassadors," or the "Throne Room," was conceived by Pedro the Cruel in 1366 and renovated by Diego Ruiz in 1427. Often hailed as the "centerpiece" of the Mudejar Palace, it was frequently used as a space for state anniversaries, celebrations, and other public events by the various rulers of the Alcázar. The striking hall features its original wooden door, horseshoe arches, and glorious tiled walls covered with floral prints and a dizzying array of geometric patterns and shapes. The star of the show, however, was the bewitching interior of the cedar wood cupola. Hundreds of circles, tears, and stars were carved into every inch of the gilded dome's belly. Inserted into each one of these crannies were hundreds of tiny sparkling mirrors.

Another important room claimed by the *Casa* was the *Cuarto del Almirante,* or the Admiral's Room. The *cuarto,* which was renovated during the time of Ferdinand and Isabella, provided shelter for multiple paintings of "National Heritage" status. The most prominent of these paintings is a piece entitled *"Las postrimerías de Fernando III el Santo"* (*The Last Days of Saint Fernando III*), by 19th century painter Virgilio Mattoni; the length of the massive canvas is equivalent to 7 pews spaced apart alone. Fernando, clothed in a pure white robe, is seen in a crumpled pile on the floor with his arms outstretched and a noose around his neck, kneeling reverently before a priest holding up the body of Christ. Other paintings found in the hall include *The Capture of Loja by Fernando el Católico,* a Eusebio Valldeperas original, Alfonso Grosso's *The Inauguration of the Latin American Exhibition of 1929,* and the full-color portraits of Maria Cristina de Napoles and Fernando VII, painted by Carlos Blanco.

When Columbus returned from his historic voyage in March of 1493, he was still under the impression that he had landed in either China or Japan. Nonetheless, he needed to secure funds and resources for a second voyage to further his research into the foreign terrains, but acquiring said funds was bound to be a challenge. Little had gone according to plan in his first voyage – not only did he sink 1 of the 3 ships entrusted to him, the small mound of gold and other material items he managed to bring back to Seville left the royals unimpressed.

It was in the *Cuarto del Almirante* that Columbus proposed to Isabella the idea and terms regarding a second voyage. As expected, Isabella was hesitant about sponsoring an even costlier expedition, especially given the unpredictability of profits and results, but by discussing and utilizing the small band of addled natives he had dragged home, Columbus was able to convince the queen to fund the trip. It helped that the relationship Columbus forged with the queen extended beyond the realms of business, as he also happened to be close friends with her. In the end, the adventurer was so persuasive that he was set to captain the largest colonization and evangelization project the West had ever known. Accompanying him to his new settlement on Hispaniola were 17 vessels packed with over 1,000 Spaniards, not to mention hordes of domesticated horses, pigs, and cattle.

Emanuel Gottlieb Leutze's painting of Columbus before Queen Isabella

When one of Columbus' brothers returned from one of his escapades along the Caribbean, he brought with him a peculiar-looking creature. It was a small, lizard-like beast, with black and brown scales, a glossy set of beady, milky eyes, short, stubby legs, jagged, sharp teeth, and a long tail. The Floridian tribespeople who sold the creature to him in exchange for a silver button had their own name for the baby animal, but the Spaniards called it the *"croca De Leons,"* or a "creature of De Leon," as a tribute to one of their captains. The creature was originally gifted to Columbus, who carried his prized pet everywhere in his satchel, but he later re-gifted the *croca de leon* to the queen when he saw how charmed she was by the funny animal. Upon tendering his birthday present to her, the queen, who was rendered bedridden by a nasty cold, misheard the creature's name, calling it a "crocodile." Columbus never corrected her.

Isabella doted over her crocodile as if it were her own offspring, even when the animal grew to over 14 feet in length. She visited her toothy companion in his lavish pen by the Mudejar courtyard, cooing over the creature as she fed it porcupine burgers, handfuls of wild oats, and other special treats. She was often seen ambling around the Alcázar with her leashed crocodile closely in tow. The queen was also known to amuse herself by setting her crocodile loose on irritating attendants and slow-walking individuals, chuckling softly as her victims scampered away in fright.

The affection and adoration Isabella had for her beloved crocodile was reciprocated. When the queen died, the crocodile allegedly tumbled into a deep depression, refusing to eat or budge for weeks on end. He even ignored the peanut butter omelets – his favorite treat – the queen's worried attendants chucked into his pen. He even began to bask in the queen's favorite sun-kissed spot in the courtyard, waiting patiently for his friend to return. When the crocodile himself eventually passed on, the new monarchs, Joanna of Castile and Charles I, sent the beast to a taxidermist. The stuffed crocodile was then mounted onto the rafters of Isabella's favorite walkway in the Alcázar, where it continues to be displayed to this day.

The *Sala de Audiencias,* or the "Audience Hall," was converted into the Chapel of Contratacion in the mid-1500s. Crowning the chapel is a florid Gothic-style "tracery roof" with an aureate honeycomb pattern of medallions and diamonds stretching from one end to the other. Embroidered banners with the crests of celebrated Castilian admirals, such as that of Christopher Columbus, decorated the walls. In the middle of the room is a stone step attached to the wall, and above it a triptych (a relief shown on 3 panels) altarpiece entitled *"Madonna of the Seafarers/Navigators,"* designed by Alejo Fernandez between 1531 and 1536.

Mary Ann Sullivan, curator of the "Seville, Spain" page on Bluffton University's Online Journal expands on the altarpiece: "It has an unusual iconography. The Madonna shelters a group of Native Americans under her cloak; in the right foreground is a group of figures...the Holy Roman Emperor Charles V, Ferdinand and Isabella (the Catholic Kings), and members of the *Casa de la Contratacion de las Indias*; on the left, under the Madonna's right hand, are Christopher Columbus and Martin and Vicente Pinzón, who accompanied Columbus on his first voyage to the New World. Below them are the various types of vessel that made up the Spanish fleet in the early 16th century. The side panels of the triptych depict saints (San Sebastian, Santiago, Saint Telmo, and Saint John the Evangelist) particularly relevant to Spain, its monarchs, and sailors..."

Not long after the establishment of the *Armería Real* (Royal Armory) in the early 16th century, Charles V demanded the construction of the *Salón de Tapices,* otherwise known as the "Hall of Tapestries." The Flemish Renaissance paintings that adorn the beige marble walls of this brilliantly lit space are an exemplar of the bountiful riches the Crown reveled in during this era.

In early March of 1535, the emperor himself boarded one of the Spanish war vessels destined for Tunis. There, Charles and 30,000 of his men were to face off against the fierce Algerian general, Hayreddin Barbarossa, and his Turkish fleet, determined to overthrow the Ottomans and restore the Hispanic crown to its full glory. Despite the impassioned protests of his aides and advisers, Charles – as mulish as he was valiant – donned his armor and raided his personal arsenal, ready to make a stand for his empire. Not only did Charles put himself in immediate danger for the sake of his empire's future, a trait uncannily rare amongst the leaders of today, he positioned himself on the front lines, aggressively defending his men and slaughtering his enemies.

While most certainly a fearless and honorable ruler, the emperor was anything but modest. On the 5th of April in the following year, Charles commemorated his long-anticipated victory against the "infidels." To eternalize the feat, the emperor enshrined his triumphs in a vivid series of paintings that illustrated the highlights of his endeavors. Flemish painter Juan Vermeyen, who had tagged along to Tunis, was made to partner with painter, sculptor, woodcutter, stained glass specialist Pieter Coecke van Aelst. It seemed as if the confident Charles had forecasted his victory over the Ottomans all along, for Vermeyen had, from the beginning, been instructed to take exhaustive notes and produce trial sketches of their foreign foes, the extraordinary North African landscape, and the events that transpired there. Joining Vermeyen was a guild of historians and poets handpicked by Charles, also tasked with translating the emperor's exploits in Tunis into verse and prose. Their works were later reproduced in a wide range of languages, including Spanish, Latin, and French.

Vermeyen and van Aelst were grateful to have been chosen for such an august undertaking, but the road to completion was long and winding. Considering its recipient, these tapestries had to surpass imperial standards. Only a decade after Charles' victorious conquest did the pair put in the order for the luxurious cloths required for the tapestry canvases. The fabrics in question were specially woven by the masterful artisans employed in Brussel native Willem de Pannemaker's workshop.

It was Charles V's sister, Maria de Hungria, who was assigned the task of communicating with the workshop and inspecting the quality of these cloths throughout their production. Maria, being the perfectionist that she was, negotiated with the workshop for more than 24 months; only in late February of 1548 was the contract finalized. As stated by the provisions of the contract, the workshop pledged to use premier wool, artisanal "worsted" yarn from the city of Lyon, and the finest silk imported from Granada in 63 different hues. Charles himself donated the gold and silver needed for the metallic threads needed to enhance the fantastic tapestries. All in all, 7 types of thread cast from pure gold and 3 from silver were spun for His Highness.

Naturally, Charles was emotionally invested in this project, and some would say he was a little too invested. After all, this was his way of putting his stamp on history, hoping that his bravery would be remembered and marveled at by future generations. The emperor's impatience increased by the day, and in an effort to accelerate the process, Charles commanded Pannemaker to hire an extra 7 weavers to work on his tapestries around the clock. This was precisely what Pannemaker did, and with the extra hands, the intricate pieces – 12 panels in total, measuring about 600 square meters in size – were churned out in less than 8 years. Altogether, the cartoons, materials, and labor set the court back a whopping 26,000 pounds, which equates to millions when converted to modern-day currencies. This terrific treasury of tapestries can now be appreciated by the visitors of the Alcázar in the *Salón de Tapices*. Though the tapestries permanently resided in the *Salón*, they were unfurled at various Habsburg affairs and public celebrations.

Following the disastrous 9.0-magnitude earthquake that shook the neighboring city of Lisbon on the 1ˢᵗ of November in 1755, the Spanish government decided that another major round of renovations was in order. Half of the laborers were assigned to re-stabilizing foundations and sealing the cracks and damage sustained during the quake and ensuing aftershocks. The rest were expected to work on reorganizing, as well as adding to the compendium of dreamy gardens within the palatial complex, most notably the *Huerta de la Alcoba, Las Damas, Las Galeras, El Rústico,* the 18th-century *Jardin Ingles* (The English Garden), the *Jardin de los Poetas* (The Garden of the Poets), and the Grutesco Gallery, to name a few. The most noteworthy of all these gardens, past and present, is the *Jardin del Estanque,* the "Garden of the Mercury Pond." Nested in a thicket of tall, verdant trees, and fronting the Moorish loggia is a rectangular pool of twinkling water. The centerpiece of this pond is a goblet-shaped, 2-tiered fountain constructed out of volcanic stones and gritty sea gravel. Sitting atop the lower tier of the fountain is a circle of chubby cherubs with curly ringlets for hair. Below them is a circle of mythical beasts interspersed with long spouts that spurted out jets of water. Last, but not least, is the imposing bronze statue of the god Mercury depicted with his winged helmet, a gorgeous showpiece designed by 16ᵗʰ century Spanish sculptor Diego de Pesquera and cast by Sevillean metallurgist Bartolomé Morel.

Splendor aside, the noble tiled walls of the Alcázar have witnessed a number of momentous historical events throughout the centuries of its existence.

To begin with, the fortress has welcomed a number of royal babies over the years. Prince Juan of Asturias, for one, was born right inside the fortress walls on June 30, 1478. Queen Isabella and her husband, Ferdinand II of Aragon, may have already been the proud parents of four intelligent and courtly young women, but to them, Juan was nothing short of a miracle, for he was the only one of their sons to survive their childhoods, making him the long-awaited heir to the throne.

The royal couple made their glee no secret. For the next 3 days, the city was hectic with musical parades, thrilling dances, and lively festivities. Another round of celebrations transpired about a week after Juan's birth. That morning, a majestic procession, beginning from the Alcázar, marched through the Sevillean streets, the cavalcade concluding at the local cathedral. The star of the show was resting in the arms of his nurse, the swaddled darling slumbering comfortably in the shade provided by the brocade canopy of his carriage. Riding alongside the carriage were 8 guards, clad in black cloaks, on mule-back. Silver-cross-toting clergymen, a band of sharply dressed courtiers, a parade of drummers, and a trio of pages bearing gold blocks, silver coins, and other spangled trinkets on pillows followed suit. The oblivious but beloved toddler prince, whom Isabella lovingly referred to as her special "angel," continued to receive queues upon queues of visitors and well-wishers in the following months.

Infanta Maria Antonia, daughter of Elisabetta Farnese and King Felipe V, was also born in the Alcázar.

The Alcázar was also the perfect venue for all the theatrical pomp and pageantry that went into the weddings of the European royals. On the 10th of March, 1526, Emperor Charles V wedded his first cousin, Isabel of Portugal, under the glimmering golden cupola of the *Salon de Emajedores*. To say that their wedding was a spectacle would be an understatement. Guests enjoyed a marvelous variety show performed by acrobats, alchemists, dancers, musicians, troubadours, and masked mimes. Other activities included jousting, bull-running, and even a game of hunting. As dictated by tradition, the 50 participants gathered in the Hunting Courtyard before setting out into the nearby woods, which had been furnished with deer, boars, and bears, as per the emperor's request. One of the ponds in the fortress was also stocked with schools of fish imported from faraway lands, and they were later retrieved and utilized in various dishes for the wedding feast. The festivities lasted for over a week.

The Alcázar also hosted the wedding banquet for Infanta Elena, daughter of King Juan Carlos I and the Duchess of Lugo, and Jaime de Marichalar y Saenz de Tejada, son of the Count and Countess of Ripalda, in mid-March of 1995.

In 1987, UNESCO officially declared the Alcázar, along with the Seville Cathedral and the Archivo de Indias, a world heritage site. The statement issued by the organization succinctly encapsulates the significance and wondrous legacy of this one-of-a-kind fortress: "Together these 3 buildings form a remarkable monumental complex in the heart of Seville. The cathedral and the Alcázar – dating from the Reconquest of 1248 to the 16th century and imbued with Moorish influences – are an exceptional testimony to the civilization of the Almohads as well as that of Christian Andalusia..."

Alhambra in the Present

"From me you are welcomed morning and evening by the tongues of blessing, prosperity, happiness and friendship...may its eminence be upheld by the master of divine glory and the celestial throne." – Inscription found in the throne room

Slowly but steadily, the Moorish roots of the Alhambra seemed to be fading into the distance. When the Moriscos were cast out of Spain in the early 17th century, the population plunged by at least 300,000. This drastic shrink in the population would have been conducive to the lull in progress not only in Alhambra but in all of Granada. Spain had lost a vital component of its resplendent and varied culture, and the loss of the Moors sent the economy into great distress. Bit by bit, the sublime greenery in Granada turned a depressing brown; with fewer people available to tend to the farmland and vegetation in Spain, the plots of arid, sterile land multiplied. Architectural endeavors at the Alhambra were either derailed or discontinued. Resources were exhausted, and funds in Granada were at an all-time low. Many attributed the waning funds to the overambitious projects previous monarchs at Alhambra had tackled during the 16th century.

It soon became evident that the funds needed to keep the place up and running was a burden the new authorities could not afford to carry. Raising taxes, requesting loans from allied kingdoms, and other means of fund raising were no longer viable solutions. Even worse were the repeated earthquakes and aftershocks that cursed the city around this time, making completion of any of these projects difficult if not impossible.

As a result, all ongoing projects, most notably Charles V's incomplete palace, came to a stop in 1637. During this interval of neglect, the Alhambra fell into such a severe state of shambles and disrepair that it would have made both the Moorish and Castilian regents flip over in their graves. Clouds of dirt and dust hovered over unfinished sites, paint began to peel, and cracks began to form in the corners of the once-prized ceilings, walls, and fixtures. Likewise, Granada had sunk into a state of gloom.

Towards the 18th century, authorities made some efforts to reanimate the economy and public morale, and some hoped to pick up from where they had left off in Alhambra. Only a handful of these attempts would ever start, and even then, they did not go far. The only project that seemed to have picked up any sort of steam was one masterminded by Philip V. Under the king's instructions, contractors deconstructed a Moorish palace, with much of its furniture and fixtures sold off to help with the funding of the project. This was to be the new home of the king and his wife, Queen Elizabeth of Parma. Only Philip's palace and the gardens within it underwent repairs and renovations, headed by the finest artists from Italy, whereas the other areas of Alhambra remained untouched at this time.

Philip V

Picture of a vase featuring gazelles in Alhambra

Upon Philip's eventual departure, Alhambra was left in the hands of the Spanish military, which now aimed to keep the complex away from the remorseful crown's outstretched hands. This time, only the garrisons in Alcazaba, as well as the living quarters for the new governor and his men, would be maintained. The rest of Alhambra remained ignored, and it lay in ruins. Gardens were spoiled and barren, and almost every inch of the ground was caked with dung. Water no longer gurgled from the fountains, and thick layers of dead leaves, muck, and moss floated upon the foggy pools. Beggars, vagrants, thieves, smugglers, and other rogues had broken in and created hidden lairs all around Alhambra. Novelist Richard Ford mourned, "Thus bats defile abandoned castles, and the reality of Spanish criminals and beggars destroy the illusion of this fairy place of the Moors."

2 centuries later, during the height of the Napoleonic Wars, the French troops stormed into the city of Granada and claimed it as their own, using the citadel as their new military base. When Napoleon and his troops were forced to vacate the premises in 1812, the bitter general decided that his enemies deserved none of what he had worked so strenuously to achieve. With his blessings, his men wreaked havoc in Alhambra, destroying and blowing up several areas in the complex. The Torre de Siete Suelos, Torre de Agua, and Torre del Cabo de la Carrera (Tower at the End of the Street) suffered the worst of the damage, completely knocked off their

foundations.

The aftermath might have been bleaker if it were not for one bold soldier by the name of Jose Garcia. When the wounded warrior learned of Napoleon's intentions to blow up the area between the Cabo de la Carerra and the Torre de las Infantas (Tower of the Princesses), he limped towards the site and took on the bomb on his own while his comrades fled. Luckily, the soldier was able to defuse the explosive before it could detonate. A plaque that memorializes the hero's epic efforts remains in the site today.

The romanticism phenomenon that spread across the continent in the 19th century was what put Alhambra back on the map, luring in new batches of foreign peoples and travelers from near and far. In 1870, Alhambra was formally declared a national monument of Spain, and in 1984, it became one of the sites of the UNESCO World Heritages. Modern Spanish authorities do what they can to best preserve the culture through raising awareness, protective regulations, preservation tactics, and advanced restoration techniques.

Adolf Seel's late 19th century paintings of Alhambra

Today, over 2 million tourists visit Alhambra each year, all thirsting for a peek at the pride of Moorish and European culture, and the mystical magic that lives on within these extraordinary ruins.

Online Resources

Other books about Spanish history by Charles River Editors

Other books about Alhambra on Amazon

Other titles about the Alcázar of Seville on Amazon

Further Reading about the Alcázar of Seville

Corneanu, M. (2016, October 4). Alcázar of Seville. Retrieved April 10, 2018, from https://spainattractions.es/alcazar-seville/

Editors, A. H. (2017). Royal Alcázar of Seville. Retrieved April 10, 2018, from https://en.adrianohotel.com/alcazar-of-seville

Editors, E. C. (2018). Alcazar Castle of Spain: Three of the Most Magical, Spanish-Moorish Fortresses. Retrieved April 10, 2018, from https://www.exploring-castles.com/europe/spain/alcazars/

Editors, S. S. (2012, May 6). An American in Spain, part 6: Real Alcázar of Seville. Retrieved April 10, 2018, from https://skullsinthestars.com/2012/05/06/an-american-in-spain-part-6-real-alcazar-of-seville/

Editors, F. R. (2014, October 23). The Alcázar of Seville. Retrieved April 10, 2018, from https://blog.friendlyrentals.com/en/seville/general/alcazar_seville_visit-posts-114-1_3362.htm

Editors, L. P. (2016). Real Alcázar. Retrieved April 10, 2018, from https://www.lonelyplanet.com/spain/seville/attractions/real-alcazar/a/poi-sig/411802/360736

Editors, C. C. (2017, June 21). Real Alcázar de Sevilla. Retrieved April 10, 2018, from http://www.castleholic.com/2017/06/real-alcazar-de-sevilla.html

Editors, A. S. (2013, February 11). Personalities and legends that inhabited the Alcázar in Seville return to life to become night guides. Retrieved April 10, 2018, from http://www.andalusianstories.com/the-story-of-the-day/culture/news-andalusia-seville-alcazar-night-guides/

Watson, F. F. (2014, July 5). Game of Thrones Series 5: Twelve things you didn't know about the Alcazar of Seville. Retrieved April 10, 2018, from http://scribblerinseville.com/game-of-thrones-series-5-twelve-things-you-didnt-know-about-the-alcazar-of-seville/

Watson, F. F. (2015, May 17). Game of Thrones Season 5: The Water Gardens of Dorne, aka the Alcazar of Seville. Retrieved April 10, 2018, from http://scribblerinseville.com/game-of-thrones-season-5-the-water-gardens-of-dorne-aka-the-alcazar-of-seville/

Editors, S. (2011, June 27). Primera reconstrucción virtual de un corral de comedias del s. XVII. Retrieved April 10, 2018, from http://www.agenciasinc.es/Noticias/Primera-reconstruccion-virtual-de-un-corral-de-comedias-del-s.-XVII

Valdivieso, E. (2014). The Alcazar up to the nineteenth century. Retrieved April 10, 2018, from http://www.alcazarsevilla.org/history/

Elzner, S. (2017). THE REAL ALCAZAR IN SEVILLE: PALACES OF DREAMS, GARDENS OF PLEASURE. Retrieved April 10, 2018, from http://www.happinessandthings.com/real-alcazar-seville-palace-dreams-garden-pleasure/

Steves, R. (2015). Spanish History Set in Stone. Retrieved April 10, 2018, from https://www.ricksteves.com/watch-read-listen/read/articles/spanish-history-set-in-stone

Carson, B. (2016, August 16). We visited the Spanish palace used in 'Game of Thrones' and it's even more beautiful in real life. Retrieved April 10, 2018, from http://www.businessinsider.com/visit-dorne-filming-location-in-seville-spain-2016-8#dorne-may-be-the-setting-for-one-of-the-most-despised-plotlines-in-the-game-of-thrones-tv-show-but-its-also-one-of-the-most-captivating-the-fictional-region-of-westeros-is-supposed-to-be-a-place-thats-luxurious-pleasant-and-warm-a-place-where-people-enjoyed-themselves-said-frank-doelger-executive-producer-1

Editors, M. (2014, January 12). The Most Dramatic Moment of the Middle Ages! Retrieved April 10, 2018, from http://www.medievalists.net/2014/01/the-most-dramatic-moment-of-the-middle-ages/

Belfrage, A. (2017, October 5). The spurned princess. Retrieved April 10, 2018, from https://annabelfrage.wordpress.com/tag/pedro-the-cruel/

Editors, U. H. (2017, February 15). Mistresses: María de Padilla, Practical Queen of Castile. Retrieved April 10, 2018, from http://unusualhistoricals.blogspot.tw/2017/02/mistresses-maria-de-padilla-practical.html

Rodriguez, B. (2017, Spring). Competing Images Of Pedro I: López De Ayala And The Formation Of Historical Memory. Retrieved April 10, 2018, from https://muse.jhu.edu/article/669500/pdf

Kelly, A. E. (2017, September 2). The Royal Mistress Series: Eleanor de Guzmán – The murdered mistress. Retrieved April 10, 2018, from https://www.historyofroyalwomen.com/the-royal-mistresses-series/royal-mistress-series-eleanor-de-guzman-murdered-mistress/

Belfrage, A. (2016, November 20). The king, his mistress, and his wife – A Castilian 14th century soap opera. Retrieved April 10, 2018, from https://annabelfrage.wordpress.com/tag/leonor-de-guzman/

Irving, S. (2016). Seville's Islamic Heritage. Retrieved April 10, 2018, from https://archive.islamonline.net/?p=6087

Esber, R. M. (1993, January/February). The Poet-King of Seville. Retrieved April 10, 2018, from http://archive.aramcoworld.com/issue/199301/the.poet-king.of.seville.htm

Beardsley, S. (2014, May 7). Seville: Real Alcázar sheds light on Christian, Muslim history of Spanish city. Retrieved April 10, 2018, from https://www.stripes.com/travel/seville-real-alcázar-sheds-light-on-christian-muslim-history-of-spanish-city-1.281928

Editors, S. T. (2017). The Royal Alcazar: Spain's Oldest Palace. Retrieved April 10, 2018, from http://www.seville-traveller.com/alcazar-spain/

Editors, B. V. (2017, July). Alcazar of Seville: Spain's Royal Palace. Retrieved April 10, 2018, from https://www.bellavitatravels.com/blog/2017/07/alcazar-of-seville

Editors, P. C. (2017, October 28). Real Alcazar of Seville. Retrieved April 10, 2018, from https://en.patiodelacartuja.com/blog/travel-seville/real-alcazar-of-sevilla

Editors, S. E. (2017, October 30). Step Back In Time at the Alcázar Seville, Spain. Retrieved April 10, 2018, from http://www.sapphireelmtravel.com/travel-journal/alcazar-seville-spain

Ruggles, D. F. (2012, August 23). The Alcazar of Seville & Mudejar Architectures. Retrieved April 10, 2018, from http://www.gardentaining.com/LAEP2300/virtual_tours/alcazar/alcazar pano write ups/alcazar article.pdf

Editors, S. T. (2017). Seville History. Retrieved April 10, 2018, from http://www.sevillatourist.com/history.html

Editors, T. W. (2018). Alcázar of Seville. Retrieved April 10, 2018, from https://www.thousandwonders.net/Alcázar of Seville

Editors, T. L. (2016). Fascinating Cultures and Histories of Seville. Retrieved April 10, 2018, from https://www.travelandlust.com/blog/seville-andalusia

Perez-Rodriguez, J. L. (2015, March 16). Green pigments of Roman mural paintings from Seville Alcazar. Retrieved April 11, 2018, from https://www.sciencedirect.com/science/article/pii/S0169131715001180

Editors, E. T. (2017, March 7). In the footsteps of the Moors: Seville. Retrieved April 11, 2018, from http://www.e-travelmag.com/spain/moors-seville/

Editors, W. P. (2015). The Garden of Eden, Brought to Life in the Moorish Gardens of the Alcazar of Seville. Retrieved April 11, 2018, from http://www.webphoto.ro/spain/the-garden-of-eden-brought-to-life-in-the-moorish-gardens-of-alcazar-seville.html

Editors, S. R. (2016, January 8). THE ROYAL ALCAZAR IN SEVILLE, SPAIN. Retrieved April 11, 2018, from http://simplicityrelished.com/the-royal-alcazar-in-seville-spain/

Schuermann, M. (2012, December 6). PHOTOS: Seville's Beautiful Tiles. Retrieved April 11, 2018, from https://www.huffingtonpost.com/michael-schuermann/seville-tiles-photos_b_2231468.html

Editors, V. S. (2016). Seville City. Retrieved April 11, 2018, from
http://www.casanumero7.com/seville/seville.html

Editors, T. M. (2008). SEVILLE - HISTORY. Retrieved April 11, 2018, from
https://www.tripmasters.com/europe/cms/2420/Web_Content.aspx

Editors, S. C. (2016). THE ALCAZAR. Retrieved April 11, 2018, from
http://www.sevillacb.com/en/monuments/the-alcazar

Editors, D. (2017). Huerta de la Alcoba, Alcázar of Seville. Retrieved April 11, 2018, from
https://www.doaks.org/resources/middle-east-garden-traditions/catalogue/C4

Editors, D. (2017). Patio del Yeso, Alcázar of Seville. Retrieved April 11, 2018, from
https://www.doaks.org/resources/middle-east-garden-traditions/catalogue/C28

Editors, D. (2017). Patio de la Casa de Contratación, Alcázar of Seville. Retrieved April 11,
2018, from https://www.doaks.org/resources/middle-east-garden-traditions/catalogue/C9

Editors, D. (2017). Patio del Crucero, Alcázar of Seville. Retrieved April 11, 2018, from
https://www.doaks.org/resources/middle-east-garden-traditions/catalogue/C10

Editors, C. C. (2017, August 10). Los 12 personajes del Alcazar de Sevilla. Retrieved April 11,
2018, from https://conocemiciudad.com/12-personajes-alcazar-sevilla/

Editors, S. O. (2014). The Royal Alcazar palace - Seville. Retrieved April 11, 2018, from
http://www.sevillaonline.es/english/seville/alcazar-palace.htm

Curtius, Q. (2018, March 21). Reversal Of Fortune: The Fate Of Al-Mu'tamid Ibn Abbad,
Ruler Of Seville. Retrieved April 11, 2018, from https://qcurtius.com/2018/03/21/reversal-of-
fortune-the-fate-of-al-mutamid-ibn-abbad-ruler-of-seville/

Editors, E. B. (2014, December 18). Al-Mu'tamid. Retrieved April 11, 2018, from
https://www.britannica.com/biography/al-Mutamid-Abbadid-ruler-1027-1095

Editors, T. O. (2009, March 15). Water in Islamic Architecture. Retrieved April 11, 2018, from
http://throughtheoculus.blogspot.tw/2009/03/water-in-islamic-architecture.html

Editors, M. M. (2016). Http://micamara.es/real-alcazar-de-sevilla/. Retrieved April 11, 2018,
from http://micamara.es/real-alcazar-de-sevilla/

Editors, W. M. (2010, October 20). A Brief History of Seville, Spain. Retrieved April 11,
2018, from http://www.worldmonumentphotos.com/blog.php?articleID=7

Metts, S. (2016, May 31). Fernando III of Castilla: Saint, King, and Conqueror. Retrieved April 11, 2018, from https://catholicexchange.com/fernando-iii-of-castilla-saint-king-conqueror

Editors, N. (2011, April 14). St. Ferdinand III of Castile and Leon extends the Reconquista to Seville and the south of Spain. Retrieved April 11, 2018, from http://www.nobility.org/2011/04/14/st-ferdinand-iii-of-castile-and-leon-extends-the-reconquista-to-seville-and-the-south-of-spain/

Editors, J. N. (2017, May 13). It's the real deal! Visiting Real Alcazar, Seville. Retrieved April 11, 2018, from http://journeyofanomadicfamily.com/real-alcazar-seville/

Editors, E. B. (2018, January 12). Order of Santiago. Retrieved April 11, 2018, from https://www.britannica.com/topic/Order-of-Santiago

Smith, W., LLD. (2017). Collegium. Retrieved April 11, 2018, from http://penelope.uchicago.edu/Thayer/E/Roman/Texts/secondary/SMIGRA*/Collegium.html

Gould, A. (2013, May 27). The Ancient Churches of Spain. Retrieved April 11, 2018, from https://www.orthodoxartsjournal.org/the-ancient-churches-of-spain/

Editors, C. N. (2018, April 4). ST. ISIDORE OF SEVILLE. Retrieved April 11, 2018, from https://www.catholicnewsagency.com/saint/st-isidore-of-seville-425

Editors, A. (2013). Seville City - City Walls and Gates. Retrieved April 11, 2018, from http://www.andalucia.com/cities/seville/muralla.htm

Bellos, A. (2015, February 10). Muslim rule and compass: The magic of Islamic geometric design. Retrieved April 11, 2018, from https://www.theguardian.com/science/alexs-adventures-in-numberland/2015/feb/10/muslim-rule-and-compass-the-magic-of-islamic-geometric-design

Williamson, A. (2017). The Art of Arabesque. Retrieved April 11, 2018, from http://artofislamicpattern.com/resources/introduction-to-islimi/

Reach, Z. (2017, February 13). THE SCAFFOLDING JOURNAL – THE HISTORY OF SCAFFOLDS. Retrieved April 11, 2018, from http://blog.oasismetal.net.ae/scaffolding-journal-history-scaffolds/

Editors, P. W. (2015, November 14). The Poet-King of Seville. Retrieved April 12, 2018, from https://postcardwritings.wordpress.com/2015/11/14/the-poet-king-of-seville/

Editors, A. A. (2015, August 5). Arab Spain's Poet King. Retrieved April 12, 2018, from http://www.arabamerica.com/arab-spains-poet-king/

Editors, E. B. (2014, April 17). Almoravids. Retrieved April 12, 2018, from
https://www.britannica.com/topic/Almoravids

Editors, A. (2015). ALMORAVIDS AND ALMOHADS: 11TH TO 13TH CENTURIES.
Retrieved April 12, 2018, from
http://www.andalucia.com/spainsmoorishhistory/almoravidsandalmohads.htm

Editors, T. M. (2001, October). The Art of the Almoravid and Almohad Periods (ca. 1062–
1269). Retrieved April 12, 2018, from https://www.metmuseum.org/toah/hd/almo/hd_almo.htm

Bloom, J. M. (2012, January 2). The Masterpiece Minbar. Retrieved April 12, 2018, from
http://islamic-arts.org/2012/the-masterpiece-minbar/

Editors, D. I. (2015). The Muslim West. Retrieved April 12, 2018, from
http://www.discoverislamicart.org/gai/ISL/page.php?theme=4

Editors, A. N. (2011). Mezquita de Sevilla. Retrieved April 12, 2018, from
https://archnet.org/sites/2753/media_contents/2124

Garcia, M. (2013, April 3). Patio de la casa de contratación de Sevilla. Retrieved April 12,
2018, from http://www.paisajistasmarbella.com/2013/04/patio-de-la-casa-de-contratacion-de-
sevilla/

Editors, D. (2018). What is the Royal Alcazar of Seville? Retrieved April 12, 2018, from
https://www.dosde.com/discover/en/the-royal-alcazar-of-seville/

Editors, E. W. (2017, March 12). Palacio Gótico. Retrieved April 12, 2018, from
https://es.wikipedia.org/wiki/Real_Alcázar_de_Sevilla#Palacio_Gótico

Cárdenas, M. (2014). Palacio Gótico del Alcázar de Sevilla. Retrieved April 12, 2018, from
https://serturista.com/espana/palacio-gotico-del-alcazar-de-sevilla/

Tatford, P. (2015, December 21). Seville - The Alcázar Royal Palace. Retrieved April 12,
2018, from https://www.spain-holiday.com/Seville-city/articles/seville-the-alcazar-royal-palace

Sullivan, M. A. (2005). El Alcázar--page 2 (of nine pages): Exterior facade, Palacio del Rey
Don Pedro (King Don Pedro's Palace). Retrieved April 12, 2018, from
https://www.bluffton.edu/homepages/facstaff/sullivanm/spain/seville/alcazar/alcazar2.html

Editors, E. W. (2016, December 28). Patio de la Montería. Retrieved April 12, 2018, from
https://es.wikipedia.org/wiki/Patio_de_la_Montería

Watson, F. F. (2016, February 17). Seville's Most Beautiful Palace. Retrieved April 12, 2018,
from http://www.thespainscoop.com/the-alcazar-real-of-seville/

Editors, D. I. (2016). Seville Citadel. Retrieved April 12, 2018, from
http://www.discoverislamicart.org/database_item.php?id=monument;ISL;es;Mon01;26;en

Lorente, V. L. (2014, June). Reales Alcázares de Sevilla. Retrieved April 12, 2018, from
http://www.arteguias.com/alcazar/realesalcazaressevilla.htm

Editors, E. W. (2018, February 8). Patio del León. Retrieved April 12, 2018, from
https://es.wikipedia.org/wiki/Patio_del_León

Editors, E. W. (2018, January 2). Puerta del León (Real Alcázar de Sevilla). Retrieved April
12, 2018, from https://es.wikipedia.org/wiki/Puerta_del_León_(Real_Alcázar_de_Sevilla)

Editors, F. P. (2017, November 13). Peter of Castile Biography. Retrieved April 12, 2018, from
https://www.thefamouspeople.com/profiles/peter-of-castile-6886.php

Editors, S. D. (2009, September 3). Alcázar (3): La Sala de la Justicia. Retrieved April 13,
2018, from http://sevilladailyphoto.blogspot.tw/2009/09/el-mes-del-alcazar-3-la-sala-de-la.html

Editors, T. S. (2003, October). Royal Palace in Sevilla - The Courtyard of the Maidens.
Retrieved April 13, 2018, from http://www.travelinginspain.com/sevilla/Doncellas.htm

Editors, E. W. (2018, January 23). María de Padilla. Retrieved April 13, 2018, from
https://es.wikipedia.org/wiki/María_de_Padilla

Editors, S. P. (2014, November 10). Baños de María de Padilla (Sevilla). Retrieved April 13,
2018, from https://sevillapedia.wikanda.es/wiki/Baños_de_María_de_Padilla_(Sevilla)

Editors, T. B. (2011, September 27). Baños de María Padilla. Real Alcázar de Sevilla.
Retrieved April 13, 2018, from http://tectonicablog.com/?p=37919

Editors, R. S. (2012, January 16). El Baño de María Padilla. Retrieved April 13, 2018, from
http://descubriendosevilla2012.blogspot.tw/2012/01/el-bano-de-maria-padilla.html

Editors, E. (2011). Fadrique Alfonso of Castile. Retrieved April 13, 2018, from
http://enacademic.com/dic.nsf/enwiki/1309724

Editors, V. A. (2008). Gothic Art (c.1150-1375). Retrieved April 13, 2018, from
http://www.visual-arts-cork.com/history-of-art/gothic.htm

Editors, O. R. (2014). Cristóbal de Augusta. Retrieved April 13, 2018, from
http://www.oxfordreference.com/view/10.1093/oi/authority.20110803095434213

Editors, A. T. (2018). MAIOLICA GRIGIO. Retrieved April 13, 2018, from
https://www.artistictile.com/maiolica-grigio-cmaigrg8

Sullivan, M. A. (2005). El Alcázar--page 9 (of nine pages): Palacio Gótico (also known as the Halls of Charles V). Retrieved April 13, 2018, from https://www.bluffton.edu/homepages/facstaff/sullivanm/spain/seville/alcazar/alcazar9.html

Nelson, L. H. (2013). The Avignon Papacy, 1305-1378. Retrieved April 13, 2018, from http://www.vlib.us/medieval/lectures/avignon.html

Eisenberg, D. (2016). Slavery. Retrieved April 13, 2018, from http://users.ipfw.edu/jehle/deisenbe/Enc_of_Medieval_Iberia/Slavery.pdf

Editors, E. W. (2017, November 11). María Fernández Coronel. Retrieved April 13, 2018, from https://es.wikipedia.org/wiki/María_Fernández_Coronel

Editors, S. (2018). Joaquin Sorolla y Bastida. Retrieved April 13, 2018, from http://www.sothebys.com/en/auctions/ecatalogue/lot.60.html/2013/19th-century-european-art-n08989

Editors, I. S. (2018). Royal Alcazar of Seville. Retrieved April 13, 2018, from https://www.inspain.org/en/extraSites/royalalcazarofsevilleartisticintroduction.asp

Editors, I. S. (2018). Historical Introduction. Retrieved April 13, 2018, from https://www.inspain.org/en/extraSites/royalalcazarofsevillehistoricalintroduction.asp

Editors, M. P. (2017). LOS TAPICES DEL ALCAZAR DE SEVILLA. Retrieved April 13, 2018, from https://marcopolito56.wordpress.com/pueblos-con-encanto/los-tapices-del-alcazar-de-sevilla/

Editors, T. F. (2017). The Conquest of Tunis series. Retrieved April 13, 2018, from http://tapestries.flandesenhispania.org/index.php/The_Conquest_of_Tunis_series

Cavendish, R. (2003, January). The Casa de Contratacion Established in Seville. Retrieved April 13, 2018, from https://www.historytoday.com/richard-cavendish/casa-de-contratacion-established-seville

Editors, E. B. (2007, March 22). Casa de Contratación. Retrieved April 13, 2018, from https://www.britannica.com/topic/Casa-de-Contratacion

Gutierrez, S. (2017, February 14). El Alcázar de Sevilla, un Palacio Real de ensueño. Retrieved April 13, 2018, from http://www.elpasodelhombre.com/el-alcazar-de-sevilla-un-palacio-real-de-ensueno/

Editors, L. S. (2014, May 30). Reales Alcázares de Sevilla, -IV. Antigua Casa de la Contratación, Cuarto del Almirante, Sala de Audiencias y Sala de los Abanicos. Retrieved April

13, 2018, from http://leyendasdesevilla.blogspot.tw/2014/05/reales-alcazares-de-sevilla-iv-antigua.html

Martin, J. X. (2017). The Columbus Crocodile. Retrieved April 13, 2018, from http://jxmartin.com/Joseph_X._Martin/Columbus_Crocodile.html

Minster, C. (2017, September 2). The Second Voyage of Christopher Columbus. Retrieved April 13, 2018, from https://www.thoughtco.com/the-second-voyage-of-christopher-columbus-2136700

Sullivan, M. A. (2005). El Alcázar--page 3 (of nine pages): Chapel of the Casa de la Contratación and other details. Retrieved April 13, 2018, from https://www.bluffton.edu/homepages/facstaff/sullivanm/spain/seville/alcazar/alcazar3.html

Editors, G. T. (2018). Alcázar of Seville. Retrieved April 13, 2018, from http://www.gameofthronesspain.com/film-location/alcazar-of-seville.php

Szalay, J. (2017, September 20). Amerigo Vespucci: Facts, Biography & Naming of America. Retrieved April 13, 2018, from https://www.livescience.com/42510-amerigo-vespucci.html

Navarro, J. A. (2009, December 12). Hall of Ambassadors, Alcazar of Sevilla. Retrieved April 13, 2018, from https://www.360cities.net/image/hall-of-ambassadors-sevilla

Editors, F. H. (2015, April 10). Juan, Prince of Asturias. Retrieved April 13, 2018, from https://thefreelancehistorywriter.com/2015/04/10/juan-prince-of-asturias/

Editors, U. M. (2017). Real Alcázar. Retrieved April 13, 2018, from http://unesco.urbanismosevilla.org/unesco/en/heritage/humanidad/real-alcázar

Casas, C. (2015, May 21). The Birth of Philip II of Spain. Retrieved April 13, 2018, from https://tudorsandotherhistories.wordpress.com/category/isabella-of-portugal/

Editors, B. N. (2006). Royal Wedding in a Palace. Retrieved April 13, 2018, from http://babelnet.sbg.ac.at/themepark/castle/wedding_page.htm

Editors, U. (2018). Cathedral, Alcázar and Archivo de Indias in Seville. Retrieved April 13, 2018, from https://whc.unesco.org/en/list/383

Maugham, W. S. (2015). *The Land of The Blessed Virgin: Sketches and Impressions in Andalusia*. Simon & Schuster.

Ruiz, A. (2007). *Vibrant Andalusia: The Spice of Life in Southern Spain*. Algora Publishing.

Villalon, A., & Kagay, D. (2017). *To Win and Lose a Medieval Battle: Nájera (April 3, 1367), A Pyrrhic Victory for the Black Prince.* BRILL.

Further Reading about Alhambra

Alkhateeb, Firas. "GRANADA – THE LAST MUSLIM KINGDOM OF SPAIN." *Lost Islamic History.* Lost Islamic History, Ltd., 1 Jan. 2013. Web. 3 Apr. 2017. <http://lostislamichistory.com/granada-the-last-muslim-kingdom-of-spain/>.

Hadley-Ives, Eric, and Chun-Chi Hadley-Ives. "Alhambra." *History Lines.* History Lines, 2013. Web. 3 Apr. 2017. <http://www.historylines.net/history/spain/alhambra.html>.

Lopez, J. Bermudez, PhD. "Architectural history." *Islamic Arts & Architecture.* Islamic Arts & Architecture, 17 Mar. 2013. Web. 3 Apr. 2017. <http://islamic-arts.org/2013/the-alhambra/>.

Authors, BBC. "Muslim Spain (711-1492)." *BBC UK.* BBC, 4 Sept. 2009. Web. 3 Apr. 2017. <http://www.bbc.co.uk/religion/religions/islam/history/spain_1.shtml>.

Kim, YunHee. "Islamic Spain (711-1492)." *Academia.* Academia, Ltd., 2014. Web. 3 Apr. 2017. <http://www.academia.edu/9105793/Islamic_Spain_711-1492>.

"Epigraphic poems." *Alhambra Granada.* Area25 IT S.C.A, 2017. Web. 3 Apr. 2017. <https://www.alhambradegranada.org/en/info/epigraphicpoems.asp>.

Mirmobiny, Shadieh. "The Alhambra." *Khan Academy.* Khan Academy Organization, 2014. Web. 3 Apr. 2017. <https://www.khanacademy.org/humanities/ap-art-history/early-europe-and-colonial-americas/ap-art-islamic-world-medieval/a/the-alhambra>.

Editors, Alhambra de Granada. "Historical introduction." *Alhambra de Granada.* Area25 IT S.C.A, 2017. Web. 3 Apr. 2017. <https://www.alhambradegranada.org/en/info/historicalintroduction.asp>.

Chapman, Sukie. "The Alhambra: A Pearl Set in Emeralds." *Great Rail Journeys Magazine.* Great Rail Journeys, Ltd., 10 Feb. 2015. Web. 3 Apr. 2017. <https://www.greatrail.com/the-journey-blog/2015/february/the-alhambra-a-pearl-set-in-emeralds/>.

Editors, Expatica. "Will Alhambra be eighth Wonder of the World?" *Expatica.* Expatica Communications BV, 30 Apr. 2007. Web. 3 Apr. 2017. <http://www.expatica.com/es/news/Will-Alhambra-be-eighth-Wonder-of-the-World_144993.html>.

Editors, New World Encyclopedia. "Umayyad conquest of Hispania." *New World Encylopedia.* MediaWiki, 24 Feb. 2009. Web. 3 Apr. 2017. <http://www.newworldencyclopedia.org/entry/Umayyad_conquest_of_Hispania>.

Editors, Alhambra de Granada. "Origins of Granada." *Alhambra de Granada.* Area25 IT S.C.A, 2017. Web. 3 Apr. 2017. <https://www.alhambradegranada.org/en/info/originsofgranada.asp>.

Authors, Spanish Town Guides. "History of Granada." *Spanish Town Guides.* Spanish Town Guides, Ltd., 2011. Web. 3 Apr. 2017. <http://www.spanish-town-guides.com/Granada_History.htm>.

Editors, Love Granada. "Granada History - Alhambra, Arab Conquest and Catholic Monarchs." *Love Granada.* Love Granada, Ltd., 2008. Web. 3 Apr. 2017. <http://www.lovegranada.com/granada/history/>.

Carr, K. E. "Who were the Visigoths?" *Quatr.Us Study Guides.* Quatr.Us, Apr. 2016. Web. 3 Apr. 2017. <http://quatr.us/medieval/history/earlymiddle/visigoths.htm>.

Editors, Spain Then and Now. "Visigoths in Spain." *Spain Then and Now.* Spain Then and Now, 2009. Web. 4 Apr. 2017. <http://www.spainthenandnow.com/spanish-history/visigoths-in-spain/default_154.aspx>.

Editors, Encyclopedia Britannica. "Ṭāriq ibn Ziyād." *Encyclopedia Britannica.* Encyclopedia Britannica, Inc., 20 Oct. 2015. Web. 4 Apr. 2017. <https://global.britannica.com/biography/Tariq-ibn-Ziyad>.

Editors, New World Encyclopedia. "Berber." *New World Encylopedia.* MediaWiki, 14 Dec. 2016. Web. 4 Apr. 2017. <http://www.newworldencyclopedia.org/entry/Berber>.

Editors, Islamic History. "Islamic Golden Age." *Islamic History.* Islamic History, Ltd., 2015. Web. 4 Apr. 2017. <http://islamichistory.org/islamic-golden-age/>.

Editors, Spain Then and Now. "Visigoths and Unity." *Spain Then and Now.* Spain Then and Now, 2009. Web. 4 Apr. 2017. <http://www.spainthenandnow.com/spanish-history/visigoths-and-unity/default_156.aspx>.

Sterns, Olivia. "Muslim inventions that shaped the modern world." *CNN.* Turner Broadcasting System, Inc., 29 Jan. 2010. Web. 4 Apr. 2017. <http://edition.cnn.com/2010/WORLD/meast/01/29/muslim.inventions/>.

Editors, Muslim Press. "Inventions in the medieval Islamic world." *Muslim Press.* News CMS, 31 Oct. 2015. Web. 4 Apr. 2017. <http://www.muslimpress.com/Section-islam-22/82761-inventions-in-the-medieval-islamic-world>.

Green, David B. "This Day in Jewish History 1066: Massacre in Granada, Spain." *Haaretz.* Haaretz Daily Newspaper, Ltd., 30 Dec. 2012. Web. 4 Apr. 2017.

<http://www.haaretz.com/jewish/this-day-in-jewish-history/1066-massacre-in-granada-spain.premium-1.490809>.

Hattstein, Markus. "History of the Nasrids of Granada." *Islamic Arts & Architecture*. Islamic Arts & Architecture, 8 Sept. 2011. Web. 4 Apr. 2017. <http://islamic-arts.org/2011/history-of-the-nasrids-of-granada/>.

Editors, Granada Info. "Alcazaba." *Granada Info*. Granada Info, Ltd., 2 Mar. 2017. Web. 5 Apr. 2017. <http://granadainfo.com/alhambra/alcazaba.htm>.

Editors, Traveler's Point. "How lazily the sun..." *Traveler's Point*. Blogspot, 28 July 2015. Web. 5 Apr. 2017. <http://travelquotes.travellerspoint.com/post/125280661891/how-lazily-the-sun-goes-down-in-granada-it-hides>.

Editors, Granada Info. "Torre de la Vela." *Granada Info*. Granada Info, Ltd., 2 Mar. 2017. Web. 5 Apr. 2017. <http://granadainfo.com/alhambra/vela.htm>.

Authors, Ronda Today. "ANTEQUERA'S ALCAZABA FORTRESS." *Ronda Today*. WordPress, 8 Mar. 2016. Web. 5 Apr. 2017. <http://www.rondatoday.com/antequeras-alcazaba-fortress/>.

Authors, Garden Visit. "Alhambra." *Garden Visit: The Garden Guide*. Garden Visit, Ltd., 2013. Web. 5 Apr. 2017. <http://www.gardenvisit.com/gardens/alhambra>.

Editors, Alhambra de Granada. "Hall of the Kings." *Alhambra de Granada*. Area25 IT S.C.A, 2017. Web. 5 Apr. 2017. <https://www.alhambradegranada.org/en/info/nasridpalaces/hallofthekings.asp>.

Wacks, David A. "Ziyad ibn 'Amir al-Kinani: Popular Andalusi literature and the Arthurian tradition." *David A. Wacks*. WordPress, 21 Apr. 2015. Web. 5 Apr. 2017. <https://davidwacks.uoregon.edu/tag/alhambra/>.

Authors, Alhambra Patronato. "The Partal." *Alhambra Patronato*. Patronato de la Alhambra y Generalife, 2015. Web. 6 Apr. 2017. <http://www.alhambra-patronato.es/index.php/The-Partal/170 M5d637b1e38d/0/>.

"THE SECRETS OF THE ALHAMBRA PALACE: WATER." *Piccavey*. Piccavey, Ltd., 22 Oct. 2016. Web. 6 Apr. 2017. <https://www.piccavey.com/secrets-alhambra-palace-water/>.

Authors, Spain Then and Now. "Alhambra: Poetry and Arabesque." *Spain Then and Now*. Spain Then and Now, 2009. Web. 6 Apr. 2017. <http://www.spainthenandnow.com/spanish-architecture/alhambra-poetry-and-arabesque/default_125.aspx>.

Editors, The Independent. "After 650 years, the wisdom of the Alhambra is revealed." *The Independent Online.* Associated Newspapers, Ltd., 30 Mar. 2009. Web. 6 Apr. 2017. <http://www.independent.co.uk/news/world/europe/after-650-years-the-wisdom-of-the-alhambra-is-revealed-1658050.html>.

Authors, Lonely Planet. "Alhambra." *Lonely Planet.* Lonely Planet, Ltd., 2014. Web. 6 Apr. 2017. <https://www.lonelyplanet.com/spain/granada/attractions/alhambra/a/poi-sig/430192/360733>.

Authors, Alhambra Patronato. "THE CHAMBER OF THE AMBASSADORS." *Alhambra Patronato.* Patronato de la Alhambra y Generalife, 2014. Web. 6 Apr. 2017. <http://www.alhambra-patronato.es/index.php/The-Chamber-of-the-Ambassadors/149 M5d637b1e38d/0/>.

Editors, Edward II. "Chaos in Castile and the Battle of Vega de Granada, June 1319." *Edward II.* Blogspot, 11 May 2014. Web. 6 Apr. 2017. <http://edwardthesecond.blogspot.tw/2014/05/chaos-in-castile-and-battle-of-vega-de.html>.

Editors, History Channel. "Reconquest of Spain." *History Channel.* A&E Television Networks, LLC, 2 Jan. 2015. Web. 6 Apr. 2017. <http://www.history.com/this-day-in-history/reconquest-of-spain>.

Editors, Wiki Wand. "Abu l-Hasan Ali, Sultan of Granada." *Wiki Wand.* Wikimedia Foundation, Inc., 17 Mar. 2017. Web. 6 Apr. 2017. <http://www.wikiwand.com/en/Abu_l-Hasan_Ali,_Sultan_of_Granada>.

Firas. "SPAIN'S FORGOTTEN MUSLIMS – THE EXPULSION OF THE MORISCOS." *Lost Islamic History.* Lost Islamic History, Ltd., 9 Nov. 2012. Web. 7 Apr. 2017. <http://lostislamichistory.com/spains-forgotten-muslims-the-expulsion-of-the-moriscos/>.

Ahsan, Sabera. ""Do Not Cry as a Woman For What You Could Not Defend as a Man" – Who Was the Sultana of Granada?" *Mvslim.* Mvslim, Ltd., Aug. 2016. Web. 7 Apr. 2017. <http://mvslim.com/meet-aixa-al-hurra-unconquerable-sultana-granada/>.

Editors, Wiki Wand. "Muhammad XII of Granada." *Wiki Wand.* Wikimedia Foundation, Inc., 23 Mar. 2017. Web. 7 Apr. 2017. <http://www.wikiwand.com/en/Muhammad_XII_of_Granada>.

Telushkin, Joseph. "Modern Jewish History: The Spanish Expulsion (1492)." *The Jewish Virtual Library.* American-Israeli Cooperative Enterprise, 1991. Web. 7 Apr. 2017. <http://www.jewishvirtuallibrary.org/the-spanish-expulsion-1492>.

Bale, Jeffrey. "Tales of the Alhambra." *Jeffrey Bale's World of Gardening.* Blogspot, 16 Mar.

2012. Web. 7 Apr. 2017. <http://jeffreygardens.blogspot.tw/2012/03/tales-of-alhambra.html>.

Editors, Spain Then and Now. "Granada from the 17th to 20th Century." *Spain Then and Now*. Spain Then and Now, 2009. Web. 7 Apr. 2017. <http://www.spainthenandnow.com/spanish-history/granada-from-the-17th-to-20th-century/default_58.aspx>.

Editors, Alhambra de Granada. "Charles V Palace." *Alhambra de Granada*. Area25 IT S.C.A, 2017. Web. 7 Apr. 2017. <https://www.alhambradegranada.org/en/info/charlesvpalaceandsurroundingareas/charlesvpalac e.asp>.

Authors, Alhambra Patronato. "PALACE OF CHARLES V." *Alhambra Patronato*. Patronato de la Alhambra y Generalife, 2015. Web. 7 Apr. 2017. <http://www.alhambra-patronato.es/index.php/Palace-of-Charles-V/141 M5d637b1e38d/0/>.

Editors, Alhambra.Org. "CHARLES V PALACE." *Alhambra.Org*. Board of the Alhambra, 2014. Web. 7 Apr. 2017. <https://www.alhambra.org/en/charles-v-palace.html>.

Editors, Alhambra de Granada. "The Christian Granada." *Alhambra de Granada*. Area25 IT S.C.A, 2016. Web. 7 Apr. 2017. <https://www.alhambradegranada.org/en/info/thechristiangranada.asp>.

Claire. "La Capilla Real de Granada – The Tombs of Ferdinand, Isabella and Juana." *The Ann Boleyn Files*. WordPress, 6 May 2013. Web. 7 Apr. 2017. <https://www.theanneboleynfiles.com/la-capilla-real-de-granada-the-tombs-of-ferdinand-isabella-and-juana/>.

Editors, Piccavey. "SECRETS OF ALHAMBRA GRANADA: THE WRITING ON THE PALACE WALLS." *Piccavey*. Piccavey, Ltd., 5 Sept. 2014. Web. 7 Apr. 2017. <https://www.piccavey.com/walls-of-alhambra-granada/>.

Authors, Spain Then and Now. "Approaching the Alhambra." *Spain Then and Now*. Spain Then and Now, 2009. Web. 7 Apr. 2017. <http://www.spainthenandnow.com/spanish-architecture/approaching-the-alhambra/default_117.aspx>.

Authors, Andalucia.Com. "Granada City - The Alhambra." *Andalucia.Com*. Andalucia.Com, 2012. Web. 7 Apr. 2017. <http://www.andalucia.com/cities/granada/alhamhistory.htm>.

Authors, Grandablog.Net. "Palace of the Alhambra." *Grandablog.Net*. Grandablog.Net, 2007. Web. 7 Apr. 2017. <http://granadablog.net/tales_of_the_alhambra/index.php?chapter=2>.

O'Neill, Susi. "Battles and Bombs: The Palace of Alhambra." *Pilot Guides*. Pilot Guides, Inc.,

2014. Web. 7 Apr. 2017. <http://www.pilotguides.com/articles/battles-and-bombs-the-palace-of-alhambra/>.

Editors, Granada Info. "Granada Spain - Basic Information." *Granada Info.* Granada Info, Ltd., 22 Mar. 2016. Web. 7 Apr. 2017. <http://granadainfo.com/granadabasic.htm>.

Authors, Alhambra de Granada. "Water Tower." *Alhambra de Granada.* Area25 IT S.C.A, 2017. Web. 7 Apr. 2017.
<https://www.alhambradegranada.org/en/info/towersandhigheralhambra/watertower.asp>.

Curtis, Thomas. *The London Encyclopaedia, or Universal Dictionary of Science, Art, Literature, and Practical Mechanics: Comprising a Popular View of the Present State of Knowledge (Classic Reprint).* Vol. 11. N.p.: Forgotten , 2016. Print.

Granada, Louis Of. *The Sinner's Guide .* N.p.: CreateSpace Independent Publishing Platform , 2012. Print.

Irwin, Robert. *The Alhambra (Wonders of the World).* N.p.: Harvard U Press, 2011. Print.

"The Alhambra Palace in Granada City." *Wonders of the World.* YouTube. 27 Aug. 2016. Television.

Free Books by Charles River Editors

We have brand new titles available for free most days of the week. To see which of our titles are currently free, click on this link.

Discounted Books by Charles River Editors

We have titles at a discount price of just 99 cents everyday. To see which of our titles are currently 99 cents, click on this link.

Made in the USA
Lexington, KY
15 August 2018